THE WORLD OF

RAGGEDY

ANN

COLLECTIBLES

IDENTIFICATION & VALUES

KIM AVERY

COLLECTOR BOOKS

A Division of Schroeder Publishing Co., Inc.

The current values in this book should be used only as a guide. They are not intended to set prices, which vary from one section of the country to another. Auction prices as well as dealer prices vary greatly and are affected by condition and demand. Neither the Author nor the Publisher assumes responsibility for any losses which might be incurred as a result of consulting this guide.

Searching For A Publisher?

We are always looking for knowledgeable people considered experts within their fields. If you feel that there is a real need for a book on your collectible subject and have a large comprehensive collection, contact Collector Books.

ON THE COVER

Raggedy Ann and Andy wind-up alarm clock, metal with plastic face, 5" tall, ©1971 Bobbs-Merrill Co. Inc., West Germany. $85.00–95.00.

19" Raggedy Ann by Georgene Novelties Co. Inc., Made in USA, 1946–1963. $125.00–150.00.

Raggedy Ann and Andy watering can, 9" tall, metal, ©1973 the Bobbs-Merrill Co. Inc., by CHEIN Playthings. $30.00–35.00.

19" Raggedy Andy with paper tag, has his original box, made by Georgene Novelties Co. Inc., Made in USA, 1946–1963. $225.00–250.00 with original box.

Marcella's Raggedy Ann Doll Book, ©1940 Johnny Gruelle Co., by McLoughlin Bros. Inc. $80.00–95.00.

Cover design: Beth Summers
Book layout: Karen Geary

Printed in the U.S.A. by Image Graphics, Paducah, KY

CONTENTS

PREFACE & ACKNOWLEDGMENTS

My Raggedy adventure began on my first birthday, in 1968, when I received a Raggedy Ann doll. That doll never left my side, she went everywhere with me, even on our camping trips. She underwent many operations over the years, from the reattaching of an arm or a leg to the coat buttons my mother loving gave her for eyes, Raggedy Ann smiled throughout it all, while the heart on her chest still proudly proclaimed "I Love You." Over the years, Santa tried to entice me away from my "favorite" by leaving me new, bright, crisp Raggedys. Although I loved my new Raggedys, they never could take the place of my "favorite." So, without even realizing it, my collection had begun and continued to blossom through the years. It is still growing, as I am always looking for those ever-elusive Raggedy dolls and all of their wonderful related items. When you look at my favorite doll now, you'll see the sparkle in her coat button eyes, that I am sure comes from knowing she was the start of it all!

I would like to thank the many terrific people that I have had the wonderful experience of meeting, both in person and through the mail, that continually help fill my collection

15" Raggedy Ann, by Knickerbocker Toy Co., Inc., made in Hong Kong, circa 1968. This was my first doll; she started the whole Raggedy Ann collection. She's been camping and has lived in four different states.

with wonderful items. To my family: heartfelt appreciation to my parents, Lee and Ann Avery, who without their support, and that first Raggedy Ann doll, this book would never have been possible. Thanks to my brother, Lee, for his photography advice. For always keeping a lookout for Raggedy items to fill my collection with, a warm thanks to my brother, Mark, and his wife, Diedre, and my sister, Lisa, and her children, Lee and Jessica. My appreciation to the rest of my family and friends, far and near, for always keeping a watchful eye out for Raggedys to add to my collection! My Raggedy collection has allowed me to meet many kind and considerate people, even if only by letter, and has been, and continues to be, a truly rewarding experience.

Happy Raggedy hunting and I hope your trip through the Raggedy's world is as enjoyable as mine has been!

INTRODUCTION

Raggedy Ann and Andy, their names alone bring to mind the ever-smiling faces of the Raggedy dolls. For many years, Raggedy Ann and Andy have been a part of children's lives. They are easily recognizable with their shoe button eyes, bright yarn hair, and their heart proclaiming their love. It isn't hard to see how these dolls have retained their popularity throughout the years.

Raggedy Ann came into existence through the Raggedy Ann books which were written by Johnny Gruelle, the first of which was published in 1918. The charming adventures of Raggedy Ann sparked an immediate demand for a doll to go along with the book. In 1920, the P.F. Volland Company answered the need and began commercial production of Raggedy Ann dolls. They later included production of Raggedy Andy and some of the other popular story-book characters, such as Beloved Belindy and Uncle Clem. They continued production of the dolls through 1934.

Raggedy Ann dolls were produced by several manufacturers throughout the years: Mollye Goldman from 1935 to 1938, Georgene Novelties Company, Inc. from 1938 to 1962, Knickerbocker Toy Company from 1962 to 1982, Applause Toy Company from 1981 to present, and Playskool/Hasbro Toy Company from 1983 to present. Commercially-made dolls vary from as small as three inches to as large as six feet tall. The six-foot dolls were probably produced to be used as store displays.

Over the years, and through the various manufacturers, subtle differences in the dolls can be found. The Volland dolls have a wooden heart which was placed inside the doll's torso. Mollye dolls have a solid red heart printed on their torso. Georgene Novelties dolls, and all dolls since, have a printed heart with "I Love You" printed inside the heart.

Dolls produced by Georgene Novelties Company, Inc. are tagged on the left side of the doll's body. The very early Georgene dolls have red print on the tags for the Ann dolls and blue print for the Andy dolls. The early dolls also have the distinct black outline around the red triangle nose. Dolls produced during the mid range of Georgene's production years can be dated by their sewn-in button eyes as well as having the opening used for stuffing the doll located in the back of the doll's torso. The dolls produced in the later production years are found with permanently affixed eyes, and the yarn used for the hair is more coarse and is brighter orange and/or red in color. Some of the very last dolls to be produced by Georgene Novelties have only a flesh colored body tag with no printing on it.

Knickbocker Toy Company produced the most variety in Raggedy Ann dolls, some of which included talking Raggedy Ann dolls, marionettes, bean bag dolls, pajama bags, and musical dolls. Some of the first Knickerbocker dolls to be produced had side body tags. These dolls were typically made in New York, NY. The early dolls also have "Joy of a Toy" on the tag versus the later issues of "KTC/Knickerbocker." The earlier dolls can be found with a variety of dress patterns used for Ann's dress. After that period of time, there were two main dress patterns, which only varied around 1976 to 1978 when Ann was produced with a blue dress and red polka dots, modeled after the movie version of the doll. Knickerbocker produced dolls in many different places over the years. After New York production, dolls were produced in Japan, Hong Kong, Malaysia, Korea, and finally in Taiwan. With each different production location, the dolls appearance varied slightly. Some of the variances are quite subtle: black eye dots versus red eye dots, the texture of the yarn hair, or even the look of the face (i.e. eyelashes, nose, mouth).

The Applause Company dolls are easily recognized by their machine embroidered faces and "I Love You" hearts.

The Hasbro/Playskool dolls have printed faces with plastic affixed button eyes and a printed "I Love You" heart.

The popularity of the Raggedy Ann and Andy dolls created a virtual marketing bonanza. When people think Raggedy Ann and Andy, they picture the dolls that were manufactured, not the vast amount of Raggedy memorabilia that was produced. Raggedy Ann and Andy were depicted on a wide variety of products, both licensed and unlicensed.

This book shows some of the many different items that depicted Raggedy Ann and Andy, as well as the various dolls. Included are items that were made to be used and discarded, to items made especially for the collector. Collectors will delight in the variety of items that they will find with Raggedy Ann adorning it. This book shows some of the items that I have been collecting through the years. It seems as if the production of Raggedy items was limitless as I am continually finding new items to add to my collection.

Pricing throughout the book is given for the item pictured, and in the same condition as the item in the photo. If you have an item in the original package, it would be worth more than one that has been played with. Condition of the item is a key part to the value. Prices can vary depending on location and type of market (flea market, antique store, auction, etc.). This book is designed to give you a realistic price for the item as it is pictured in this book. When you find your item pictured in the book, determine if your item is in the same overall condition. If so, you can use the basic price listed. If your item is in lesser condition, you should deduct from listed price. If your item is in more pristine condition, you can add to the listed price. Remember, condition of an item, as well as the rarity and desirability should be considered in determining an item's value. If you have an extremely hard-to-find item that isn't in the best of condition, it still may be desirable to a collector. A more common item may only hold its value if it is in its original packaging. As always, an item is only worth what a buyer is willing to pay for it.

ACCESSORIES

"Little Raggedys" 2 piece utensil set (fork & spoon), 5½", ©Macmillan Inc., $10.00–12.00.

Raggedy Ann and Andy toy wristwatch, fully functional, ©1975 The Bobbs-Merrill Co. Inc., distributed by Marx Toys, $45.00–55.00.

Raggedy Ann and Andy desk set, molded plastic, ©1975 The Bobbs-Merrill Co. Inc., by Janex Corp., left to right: stapler, calendar, and battery-operated pencil sharpener, $20.00–25.00 for set.

ACCESSORIES

Left to right: **Raggedy Ann charm,** 1¾", metal, $10.00–12.00; **Raggedy Ann 14K gold charm,** 1¼", ©1989, $75.00–85.00; **Raggedy Ann charm,** ¾", metal, ©Bobbs-Merrill Co. Inc. $8.00–10.00; **Raggedy Ann and Andy charm,** 1¼", metal ©1973 Bobbs-Merrill Co. Inc., $12.00–15.00.

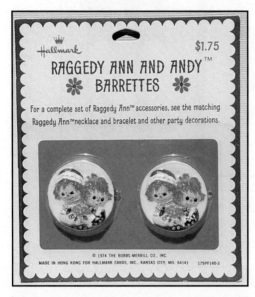

Raggedy Ann and Andy barrettes, 1¼" diameter, plastic, ©1974 Bobbs-Merrill Co. Inc., by Hallmark #175PF140-3, $25.00–30.00.

Left to right: **Raggedy Ann charm/necklace,** 2¼", plastic, ©Bobbs-Merrill Co. Inc., $12.00–16.00; **Raggedy Ann pin,** 2", plastic, ©Bobbs-Merrill Co. Inc., by Hallmark, $8.00–10.00; **Raggedy Ann pin,** 1½", plastic, ©1978 Bobbs-Merrill Co. Inc., by Hallmark #75LP243-1, $12.00–15.00.

Raggedy Ann and Andy handkerchief, 8" square, ©Bobbs-Merrill Co. Inc. by Hallmark, $10.00–15.00

Raggedy Ann and Andy metal key chains, sizes from 2" to 2½", ©Macmillan Inc., $8.00–10.00 each.

Raggedy Ann and Andy magnets, 2", plastic, ©1978, 1981 Bobbs-Merrill Co. Inc., by Pussy Willow Creations, $3.00–5.00 each.

Left: **Raggedy Ann pin-on button,** 3½" diameter, metal, "Happiness is made to be shared," ©1974 Bobbs-Merrill Co. Inc., $10.00–15.00. Right: **Raggedy Ann pin-on button,** 3½" diameter, metal, "Start each day with a smile," © 1974 Bobbs-Merrill Co. Inc., $10.00–15.00.

Left: **Raggedy Ann vinyl coin purse,** 5" x 3", ©Bobbs-Merrill Co. Inc., by Hallmark #75PF140-6, $10.00–15.00. Right: **Raggedy Ann vinyl coin purse,** 5½" x 5", ©1978 Bobbs-Merrill Co. Inc., by Pussy Willow Creations, has squeaker inside, $8.00–10.00.

Raggedy Ann and Andy handbag, 4" x 3½", vinyl handbag with metal chain, ©Bobbs-Merrill Co. Inc., by Hallmark #150PF140-5, $15.00–18.00.

Left: **Raggedy Ann and Andy Kleenex holder/purse,** 5" x 5", vinyl, ©1978, 1981 Bobbs-Merrill Co. Inc., by Pussy Willow Creations, $8.00–10.00. Right: **Raggedy Ann purse,** 4" x 3½", vinyl, ©Bobbs-Merrill Co. Inc., by Hallmark #75PF140-8, $10.00–15.00.

Top: **Raggedy Ann sewing kit,** 3" x 3½", vinyl, ©1978, 1981 Bobbs-Merrill Co. Inc., by Pussy Willow Creations, $15.00–18.00. Bottom left: **Raggedy Ann and Andy diary,** 4½" x 3½", vinyl, ©1978 Bobbs-Merrill Co. Inc., by Pussy Willow Creations, $15.00–18.00. Bottom right: **Raggedy Ann wallet,** 4" x 3½", vinyl, ©1978, 1981 Bobbs-Merrill Co. Inc., by Pussy Willow Creations, $8.00–10.00.

Raggedy Ann coin purse, 2" x 2½", vinyl, ©1975 Bobbs-Merrill Co. Inc., by Hallmark #125PF-143-1, $10.00–15.00.

Left: **Raggedy Ann barrette,** ¾" x 1½", metal, $5.00–8.00. Right: **Raggedy Andy pin,** 1¼" diameter, plastic, $3.00–5.00. Both are ©1980 Bobbs-Merrill Co. Inc., by Apple Tree Accessory.

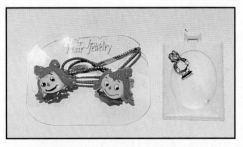

Left: **Raggedy Ann hair ornaments,** 1", plastic, $3.00–5.00. Right: **Raggedy Ann stick pin,** ¾", metal, ©1978 Bobbs-Merrill Co. Inc., $8.00–10.00.

Left: **Raggedy Ann necklace,** 1½", metal, pull the pails and Raggedy Ann climbs the chain, $15.00–20.00. Right: **Raggedy Andy necklace,** 1½", metal, "jumping jack" (push lever on side of box down and Andy jumps up), $15.00–20.00.

Raggedy Ann and Andy jewelry sets, all are metal. Top left: **Earrings**, one is Ann; the other is Andy, clip-on, 1¼", $10.00–12.00. Top right: **Oval Raggedy Ann necklace/pendant**, 2¼", $10.00–12.00. Bottom left to right: **Andy pin**, 1½", $10.00–12.00. **Ann charm**, ¾", $6.00–8.00. **Ann charm**, 1", $8.00–10.00. Below charm: **Ann ring**, ¾", $12.00–14.00. **Ann pin**, 1½", $10.00–12.00.

Left to right: **Raggedy Ann mirror**, 4½", plastic with mirror inside, ©1987 Macmillan Inc., $3.00–5.00. **Raggedy Ann comb**, 5½", plastic with vinyl holder, ©1978, 1981 Bobbs-Merrill Co. Inc., by Pussy Willow Creations, No. 11/1, $8.00–12.00. **Raggedy Ann comb**, 2½", plastic, ©1989 Macmillan Inc., $3.00–5.00.

Raggedy Ann and Andy metal lunch box, 7" x 8", ©1973 Bobbs-Merrill Co. Inc., by Aladdin Industries, includes plastic thermos, $35.00–40.00.

Raggedy Ann and Andy vinyl brunch bag, 8" square, ©1973 Bobbs-Merrill Co. Inc., by Aladdin Industries, includes plastic thermos, $75.00–80.00.

Raggedy Ann and Andy lunch box, 7" x 8½", plastic, © 1988 Macmillan Inc., includes plastic thermos, $25.00–30.00.

Raggedy Ann watch, in original case, ©1971 Bobbs-Merrill Co. Inc., by Bradley Time, $65.00–75.00.

Raggedy Ann (top) **and Raggedy Andy** (bottom) **digital quartz watch,** vinyl and plastic, ©1978, 1984 Bobbs-Merrill Co. Inc., by Nasta Ind. Inc., $35.00–40.00 each.

Raggedy Ann jewelry box, musical, plays "Raindrops Keep Falling on my Head," ©1972 Bobbs-Merrill Co. Inc., by Durham Industries, $22.00–28.00.

Raggedy Ann jewelry box, 3¼" x 5½", plastic, lift off lid, musical, plays "Candy Man," includes vinyl doll about 5" tall, ©1971 Bobbs-Merrill Co. Inc., by Durham Industries, Inc., $22.00–26.00.

Raggedy Ann compact, 2½" diameter, plastic, pressed powder, © Bobbs-Merrill Co. Inc., by Giftique, $8.00–12.00.

Raggedy Ann's Fragrance School Bus, contains one lemon hand cream, one strawberry body lotion, two bottles of cologne, ©1977 Bobbs-Merrill Co. Inc., $25.00–30.00.

Raggedy Ann perfumed dusting powder, 4 oz., ©1975 Bobbs-Merrill Co. Inc., by Giftique, $18.00–24.00 each.

Raggedy Ann six-piece soap set, six French-milled soaps, 2¼" x 1⅜", by Katherine Gray Inc., $25.00–30.00 for set.

Raggedy Ann and Andy soaps, 2¼" x 1⅜", by Katherine Gray, $8.00–12.00 each.

Raggedy Ann and Andy soaps, 3¼" x 2", by Katherine Gray, $12.00–16.00 each.

Raggedy Ann "Little Raggedys" foot jingles (left) and **Raggedy Andy "Little Raggedys" foot jingles** (right), soft fabric socks that jingle, ©1990 Macmillan Inc., by Playskool, $15.00–20.00 each.

Raggedy Ann and Andy 3-piece melamine set (divided dish, bowl, and cup), by Applause, ©1990 Macmillan Inc., $20.00–25.00. Shown in drinking cup is the Raggedy Ann and Andy 2-piece utensil set (spoon and fork), by Applause, ©1990 Macmillan Inc., $10.00–14.00.

Raggedy Ann and Andy drinking glasses, 4½" tall, five glasses in set, each has a different Raggedy character on it, ©1994 Macmillan Inc., by KIP's Japan, available only in Japan, $75.00–80.00 set. Right: Reverse side of glass shown close-up.

Left: Raggedy Ann compact, plastic, party favor, sponge and mirror inside, by Hallmark #50PF162-3. Right: Same compact with variation of colors, MIP. $15.00–18.00 each.

Raggedy Ann bubble bath puppet, 8½" tall, 12 oz. bubble bath with detachable puppet, ©1978 Bobbs-Merrill Co. Inc., by Giftique, $15.00–20.00.

Raggedy Ann cologne doll, 8" tall, plastic bottle with stryofoam/material doll, ©1977 Bobbs-Merrill Co. Inc., by Giftique, $15.00–18.00.

Raggedy Andy earring holder, 5½" tall, metal, $12.00–16.00.

Raggedy Ann and Andy wind-up alarm clock, 5½" tall, metal with plastic face, ©1971 Bobbs-Merrill Co. Inc., West Germany, $85.00–95.00.

Raggedy Andy battery-powered toothbrush, plastic, ©1973 Bobbs-Merrill Co. Inc., by Janex, $25.00–30.00.

Raggedy Ann and Andy bookends, 6" tall, ceramic with felt bottom, stamped FABIL NYC, ©Bobbs-Merrill 1976, $25.00–30.00 set.

Raggedy Ann and Andy bookends, 6" tall, papier-mache type material with felt bottom, sand filled, stamped ©1970 Bobbs-Merrill Co. Inc., world rights reserved, Determined Products Inc, $25.00–30.00 set.

Raggedy Ann and Andy bookends, 6½" tall, ceramic, sand filled with felt bottom, paper sticker "handmade in Japan," $25.00–30.00 set.

Raggedy Ann and Andy earring holders, 5¼" tall, metal, $10.00–12.00 each.

Left to right: **Raggedy Ann wallet,** 4½", vinyl, ©1989 Macmillan Inc., $10.00–12.00; **Raggedy Ann change purse,** 5", vinyl, ©1975 Bobbs-Merrill Company Inc., by Hallmark #85XPF11-7, $12.00–15.00; **Raggedy Ann change purse,** 3" square, vinyl, ©1978, 1981 Bobbs-Merrill Co. Inc., by Pussy Willow Creations, $8.00–12.00.

Raggedy Ann shower cap, 9" diameter, plastic, ©1982 Bobbs-Merrill Co. Inc., by Giftique, $8.00–10.00.

Raggedy Ann and Andy light switch cover, 5" x 3", plastic, ©Bobbs-Merrill Company Inc., $8.00–10.00.

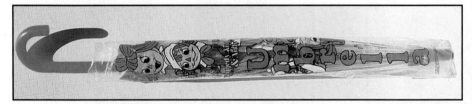

Raggedy Ann and Andy umbrella, 24" long, vinyl and metal, ©1972 Bobbs-Merrill Co. Inc., $20.00–25.00.

Raggedy Ann and Andy trash can, 13" tall, metal, ©1973 Bobbs-Merrill Co. Inc., by Cheinco (photo on right shows opposite side of trash can), $20.00–25.00.

Raggedy Ann and Andy trash can, 13" tall, metal, ©1972 Bobbs-Merrill Company Inc., by Cheinco (photo on right shows opposite side of trash can), $20.00–25.00.

Raggedy Ann and Andy trash can, 13" tall, metal, ©Bobbs-Merrill Company Inc. (photo on right shows opposite side of trash can), $25.00–30.00.

Raggedy Ann and Andy bathroom set, 3-piece plastic set consists of 10" trash can, 3" water cup, and 4" toothbrush holder, ©1988 Macmillan Inc., $20.00–25.00 for set.

Top: **Raggedy Ann belt,** vinyl belt with metal buckle with plastic Raggedy Ann insert, ©Bobbs-Merrill Co. Inc., $18.00–22.00. Bottom: **Raggedy Ann belt,** vinyl belt with metal buckle with plastic Raggedy Ann insert, ©1973 Bobbs-Merrill Co. Inc., $20.00–25.00. Both by Pyramid Belt Co. Inc., NY.

Raggedy Ann curler bag, 8½" tall x 7" round, material with cardboard insert, $30.00–35.00.

Raggedy Ann and Andy wall plaques, 10" long including ribbon, $15.00–20.00 pair.

Raggedy Ann chair, 28" tall, metal frame, vinyl seat and back, ©Bobbs-Merrill Company Inc., $55.00–60.00.

Left to right: **Raggedy Ann magnifying glass,** plastic, ©1980 Bobbs-Merrill Co. Inc., by Nasta, $10.00–12.00; **Raggedy Ann compass,** plastic and metal, ©1980 Bobbs-Merrill Co. Inc., by Nasta, $10.00–12.00; **Raggedy Ann pencil sharpener,** plastic, ©1980 Bobbs-Merrill Co. Inc., by Nasta, $10.00–12.00.

Raggedy Ann jump rope, plastic, ©Bobbs-Merrill Company Inc., by Hallmark #179PF140-7, $18.00–22.00.

Raggedy Ann clothes hanger, plastic, ©1978, 1981 Bobbs-Merrill Co. Inc., by Pussy Willow Creations, $10.00–12.00.

Left to right: **Raggedy Ann fold open comb & mirror,** 3¼", plastic, ©1989 Macmillan Inc., $8.00–10.00; **Raggedy Ann necklace,** 2", metal, $8.00–10.00; **Raggedy Ann and Andy pin,** 2", plastic, ©Bobbs-Merrill Company Inc., by Hallmark, $12.00–15.00.

Raggedy Ann "look pretty" make-up purse, 9" x 8", plastic purse type holder, ©1975 Bobbs-Merrill Co. Inc., by Giftique, $20.00–25.00.

Raggedy Andy slippers, ©1989 Macmillan Inc., $15.00–18.00.

Raggedy Ann earring holder, 6", metal, by Revere Mfg., $8.00–12.00.

Left: **Raggedy Andy wooden light switch cover,** 5½", $10.00–12.00. Right: **Raggedy Andy ceramic wall plaque,** 5½", $5.00–8.00.

Raggedy Ann and Andy inflatable dolls, 14½" Ann, 12" Andy, vinyl, $30.00–35.00 each.

Raggedy Ann pajama bag dolls, 27" long, cloth, Knickerbocker Toy Co. Inc, made in Japan, each has a different dress pattern, late 1960s, $30.00–35.00 each.

Top: **Raggedy Ann and Andy appliqué,** 3½", by Rose Import Inc., $5.00–8.00 each. Bottom: **Raggedy Ann and Andy embroidered appliqués,** 4½", by L.A. Trimming Co., $3.00–5.00 each.

Left: **Raggedy Ann and Andy appliques,** Talon® by Donahue Sales, ©1973, 1½", two in pack, $5.00–8.00. Right: **Raggedy Ann and Andy embroidered denim iron-on patches,** Embassy Trimmings, 4" x 3", $4.00–6.00 each.

Left: **Raggedy Ann and Andy buttons,** ⅝", plastic, JHB Imports, $8.00–10.00. Right: **Raggedy Ann and Andy buttons,** ⅝", Le Bouton, plastic, B. Blumenthal & Co. Inc., $8.00–10.00.

Left: **Raggedy Ann and Andy embroidered denim iron-on patches,** 4" x 3", by Embassy Trimmings, $5.00–8.00 each. Right: **Raggedy Ann and Andy iron-on patch,** 4" x 3", ©Joy Insingia Inc., $5.00–8.00 each.

Raggedy Ann and Andy figurines, plastic, by Mangelsen's, $3.00–6.00 each set.

Raggedy Ann and Andy inflatable dolls, 22" Andy, 21" Ann, ©1973 Bobbs-Merrill Co. Inc., by Ideal, $45.00–50.00 each. On right are packages for the inflatable dolls.

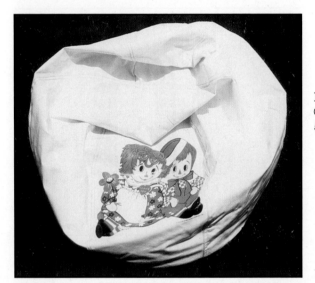

Raggedy Ann and Andy beanbag chair, vinyl, ©1975 Bobbs-Merrill Co. Inc., hard to find, $45.00–50.00.

Raggedy Ann and Andy inflatable vinyl chairs, 20" tall, made in Taiwan, very unusual, $45.00–50.00 each.

Raggedy Ann dress up n' play shoes, by Lapin, ©1972 Bobbs-Merrill Co. Inc., No. 25, $30.00–35.00.

Raggedy Ann and Andy melmac dinnerware, all are ©1969 Bobbs-Merrill Co. Inc., by Oneida Deluxe. Top left: Bowl, 6½" round, $6.00–8.00. Top right: Bowl, 4½" round, $4.00–6.00. Bottom left: Cup, 3" tall, $6.00–8.00. Bottom right: Plate, 7½" round, $6.00–8.00.

Raggedy Ann and Andy melmac dinnerware, all are ©1969 Bobbs-Merrill Co. Inc., by Oneida Deluxe. Top left: Bowl, 4½" round, $4.00–6.00. Top right: Bowl, 6½" round, $6.00–8.00. Bottom: Plate, 7½" round, $6.00–8.00.

Raggedy Ann and Andy magnetic pencil case, 8½", vinyl and plastic, ©1974 Bobbs-Merrill Co. Inc., $12.00–15.00.

Raggedy Ann wipe-off slate, plastic, slate about 7½" long, ©1978 Bobbs-Merrill Co. Inc., by Pussy Willow Creations, $15.00–18.00.

Left: **Raggedy Ann and Andy mini clipboard,** 4", plastic, ©1978 Bobbs-Merrill Co. Inc., by Pussy Willow Creations, $10.00–12.00. Right: **Raggedy Ann pencil cup,** 4", vinyl, ©1978, 1981 Bobbs-Merrill Co. Inc., by Pussy Willow Creations, $10.00–12.00.

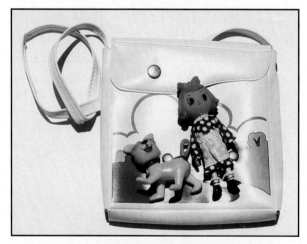

Raggedy Ann play purse, 6" square, vinyl, figurines are plastic and rubber and snap off so you can play with them, ©1980 Bobbs-Merrill Co. Inc., $12.00–16.00.

Raggedy Ann cosmetic purse, cloth purse is about 12" long, comes with two ounce hand cream and two ounce cologne, ©1977 Bobbs-Merrill Co. Inc., by Giftique, $30.00–35.00.

Raggedy Ann umbrella, 23½" tall, vinyl and metal, ©1972 Bobbs-Merrill Co. Inc., $25.00–30.00.

Raggedy Ann pajama bag dolls, 29" long, cloth, all made by Simon Simples Originals, all ©Bobbs-Merrill Co. Inc. (left and right dolls are from 1968; center doll is from 1970), $20.00–25.00 each.

Raggedy Ann and Andy pillow, 17" x 17", tagged ©1970 Bobbs-Merrill Co. Inc., printed and sewn in Japan, $20.00–25.00.

Raggedy Ann diaper stacker, 29½", cloth, by Simon Simple Originals, ©1974 Bobbs-Merrill Co. Inc., $28.00–32.00.

Raggedy Ann pillow, 16" square, tagged ©1971 Bobbs-Merrill Co. Inc., sewn in Japan, $20.00–25.00.

Raggedy Ann and Raggedy Andy pillows, 15" x 11", both made by I.S. Sutton & Sons Inc., both ©1974 Bobbs-Merrill Co. Inc., $25.00–30.00 each.

ACCESSORIES

Raggedy Ann hand towel, 16½" x 13", Raggedy Ann appliqué and "Raggedy Ann" embroidered on towel, ©1991 Macmillan Inc., available only in Japan, tag information in Japanese, $15.00–20.00.

Raggedy Ann and Andy towel, 16" x 24", ©Bobbs-Merrill Co. Inc., By Wamsutta Heritage Towels, $22.00–25.00.

Raggedy Ann and Andy bath towel, front and reverse shown, 24" x 40", ©Bobbs-Merrill Co. Inc., by Wamsutta Heritage Towels, $25.00–30.00.

Raggedy Ann and Andy wash cloth, 11½" x 12", ©Bobbs-Merrill Co. Inc., by Wamsutta Heritage Towels, $15.00–18.00.

Raggedy Ann and Andy beach towel, 26" x 50", ©1976 Bobbs-Merrill Co. Inc., by R. A. Briggs, $35.00–40.00.

Raggedy Ann and Andy cut-and-stuff dolls, 20", ©1982 Bobbs-Merrill Co. Inc., by Springs Mills Inc., $25.00–30.00 set.

Raggedy Ann and Andy dish towel, 18" long, has Ann and Andy appliqué, $18.00–22.00.

Raggedy Ann, Andy, and Arthur decorative cut-and-stuff pillow, finished size 14" square, ©1978 Bobbs-Merrill Co. Inc., by Springs Mills Inc., $15.00–18.00.

Child's shirt made from Raggedy Ann and Andy material, material is ©Bobbs-Merrill Company Inc., $8.00–12.00.

ACCESSORIES

Raggedy Ann and Andy "look-a-like" material, no markings, three different color variations, $5.00–6.00 per yard.

Raggedy Ann and Andy child's one-piece pajamas, size small, ©1980 Bobbs-Merrill Co. Inc., $8.00–10.00.

Raggedy Ann and Andy material, ©1978 Bobbs-Merrill Co. Inc., $12.00–15.00 per yard.

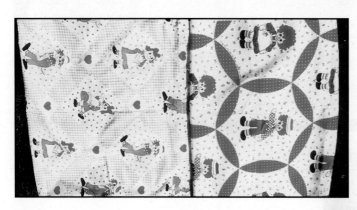

Raggedy Ann and Andy material, left is ©1982 Bobbs-Merrill Co. Inc., right is ©1978 Bobbs-Merrill Co. Inc., both by Spring Mills Inc., $12.00–15.00 per yard.

Raggedy Ann and Andy material, both are "look-a-like" type dolls, no markings, $3.00–5.00 per yard.

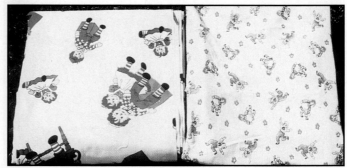

Raggedy Ann and Andy cut-and-stuff dolls, 20"
dolls, ©Bobbs-Merrill Company Inc., by Wamsutta Fabrics, $25.00–30.00 each.

Raggedy Ann and Andy material. Left: ©Bobbs-Merrill
Co. Inc., $8.00–10.00 per yard. Right: No markings on
material, $3.00–5.00 yard.

Raggedy Ann and Andy material. Left: ©1978 Bobbs-
Merrill Co. Inc., by Springs Mills Inc., $8.00–10.00 per
yard. Right: No markings, $6.00–8.00 per yard.

Left: **Raggedy Ann cut-and-stuff doll,** 16", ©1975 Bobbs-
Merrill Co. Inc., by Colorforms, $15.00–18.00. Right: **Raggedy
Andy "look-a-like" doll** to cut and stuff, 16", $5.00–6.00.

Raggedy Arthur cut-and-stuff dog, 16",
©1978 Bobbs-Merrill Co. Inc., by Springs
Mills Inc., $20.00–25.00.

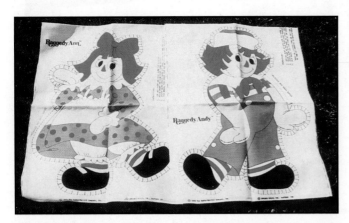

Raggedy Ann and Andy cut-and-stuff dolls, 20", ©1978 Bobbs-Merrill Co. Inc., by Springs Mills Inc., $25.00–30.00 set.

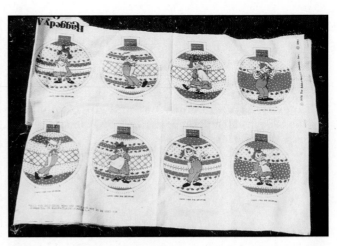

Raggedy Ann and Andy cut-and-stuff ornaments, eight in set, ©1978 Bobbs-Merrill Co. Inc., by Springs Mills Inc., $18.00–22.00.

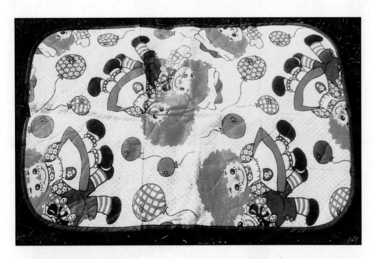

Raggedy Ann and Andy pillow sham, standard size, ©Bobbs-Merrill Company Inc., $15.00–20.00.

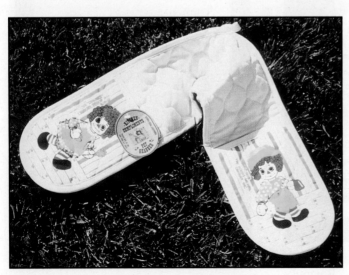

Raggedy Ann and Andy pot grabbers, 32" long, ©1976 Bobbs-Merrill Co. Inc., by Franco MFG Co. Inc., $25.00–30.00.

Raggedy Ann and Andy apron, ©1976 Bobbs-Merrill Co. Inc., $25.00–30.00.

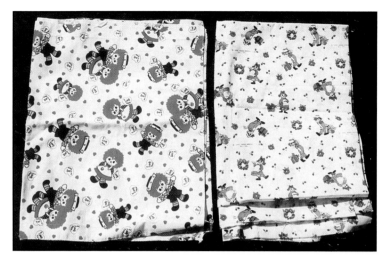

Raggedy Ann and Andy material. Left: ©Bobbs-Merrill Company Inc., $12.00–15.00 per yard. Right: ©1978 Bobbs-Merrill Co. Inc., $12.00–15.00 per yard.

Child's Raggedy Ann dress, size 5, ©1989 Macmillan Inc., $15.00–20.00.

Raggedy Ann and Andy pillow shams, standard size, ©1980 Bobbs-Merrill Co. Inc., by Montgomery Ward, $25.00–30.00 each.

Raggedy Ann and Andy receiving blanket, 30" x 40", ©Bobbs-Merrill Co. Inc., $20.00–25.00.

Raggedy Ann and Andy baby blanket, 34" x 48", ©Bobbs-Merrill Company Inc., $15.00–20.00.

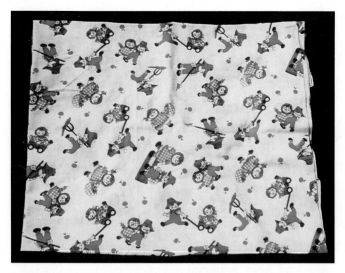

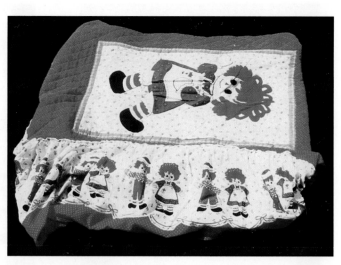

Raggedy Ann and Andy look-a-like material, by M. Lowenstein & Sons Inc., $3.00–5.00 per yard.

Raggedy Ann bedspread, twin size, ©1978 Bobbs-Merrill Co. Inc., $35.00–40.00.

Left: **Raggedy Ann and Andy pillowcase,** 42" x 36", by Wamsutta, ©1969 Bobbs-Merrill Co. Inc., in original package, $18.00–20.00. Right: **Raggedy Ann and Andy pillowcase,** same as one on left except this one is out of the package, $10.00–12.00.

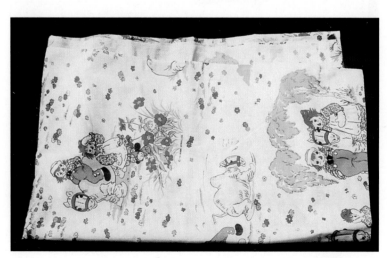

Raggedy Ann and Andy sheet, matches the pillowcases in above photos, by Wamsutta, ©1969 Bobbs-Merrill Co. Inc., $18.00–20.00.

Raggedy Ann and Andy bedspread, twin size, ©Bobbs-Merrill Company Inc., by Wamsutta, $20.00–25.00.

Raggedy Ann and Andy bedspread, twin size, ©Bobbs-Merrill Company Inc., $20.00–25.00.

Raggedy Ann and Andy pillowcase, standard size, ©Bobbs-Merrill Company Inc., by Wamsutta, $8.00–10.00.

Raggedy Ann and Andy twin sheet, ©Bobbs-Merrill Company Inc., by Pacific, $12.00–15.00.

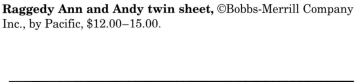

Raggedy Ann and Andy pillowcase, matches sheet in above photo, ©Bobbs-Merrill Company Inc., by Pacific, $8.00–10.00.

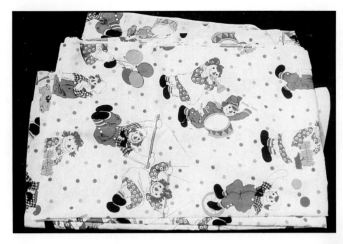

Raggedy Ann and Andy twin sheet, ©Bobbs-Merrill Company Inc., by Pacific, $12.00–15.00.

Raggedy Ann and Andy standard pillow case, matches sheet in above photo, ©Bobbs-Merrill Company Inc., by Pacific, $8.00–10.00.

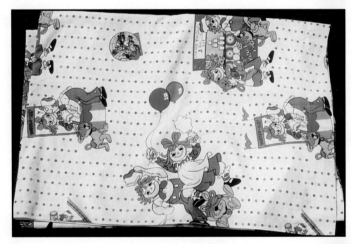

Raggedy Ann and Andy twin sheet, ©1981 Bobbs-Merrill Co. Inc., by Wamsutta, $12.00–15.00.

Raggedy Ann and Andy standard pillow case, ©1980 Bobbs-Merrill Co. Inc., $8.00–10.00.

Raggedy Ann and Andy standard pillow case, ©Bobbs-Merrill Company Inc., by Sears, Roebuck and Co., $8.00–10.00.

Raggedy Ann and Andy twin bedspread, matches pillow case in left photo, ©Bobbs-Merrill Company Inc., by Wamsutta, $30.00–35.00.

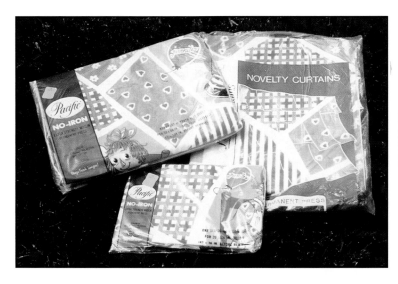

Raggedy Ann and Andy twin sheet, standard pillow case, and matching curtains, all still in original packages, ©Bobbs-Merrill Company Inc., by Pacific, $20.00–25.00 each.

Raggedy Ann and Andy vinyl piece, probably for use as a tablecloth, no markings, $10.00–12.00 per yard.

BANKS

Raggedy Ann and Andy banks, 6" tall, papier-maché type material, marked "Japan," $10.00–15.00 for pair.

Raggedy Ann and Andy ceramic banks, 5" tall, stamped 4T-2844, paper sticker "Brinn's Pittsburgh PA, made in Japan," $25.00–30.00 for pair.

Raggedy Ann savings bank with real yarn hair, 6" tall, ceramic, © 1981 Bobbs-Merrill Co. Inc., by Pussy Willow Creations, No 91/21, Made in Taiwan, $20.00–25.00. Right photo shows the box.

Left: **Raggedy Andy bank,** 8" tall, ceramic, no markings, $10.00–15.00. Right: **Raggedy Ann bank,** 4½" tall, plastic, © 1974 Bobbs-Merrill Co. Inc., Made in Hong Kong by Aviva, $10.00–14.00.

Raggedy Ann and Andy bank, 6" tall sitting, papier-maché, paper sticker "Hand made in Japan," stamped "©1971 the Bobbs-Merrill Co. Inc., world rights reserved, Determined Productions Inc.," $20.00–25.00.

Left to right: **Raggedy Ann ceramic bank,** 4½" tall, no markings; **Raggedy Ann bank,** 7" tall, ceramic, paper sticker "Pacific Import Japan"; **Raggedy Andy ceramic bank,** 7" tall, paper sticker "Pacific Imports Japan"; **Raggedy Andy ceramic bank,** 4¼" tall, no markings. Small banks: $8.00–12.00 each. Larger banks: $15.00–18.00 each.

Raggedy Ann and Andy banks, 7" tall, ceramic, sticker with Lefton trademark "exclusives Japan," $10.00–15.00 pair.

Raggedy Ann and Andy musical bank, 4½" tall, ceramic, no markings, plays music when coin is inserted, $15.00–20.00.

Left: **Raggedy Ann bank,** 10" tall, ceramic with yarn hair, stamped, ©R.S. 1972, $10.00–15.00. Right: **Raggedy Ann bank,** 14½" tall, ceramic with yarn hair, no markings, $20.00–25.00.

Left: **Raggedy Andy bank,** 14½" tall, ceramic with yarn hair, stamped "Japan," $20.00–25.00. Right: **Raggedy Andy bank,** 10" tall, ceramic with yarn hair, stamped, ©R.S. 1972, $10.00–15.00.

Raggedy Ann bank, 6" tall, ceramic with lavender yarn hair, material legs, stamped "Japan," $8.00–12.00.

Raggedy Ann bank, 7¼" tall, ceramic with yarn hair, stamped "Japan," $8.00–12.00.

Raggedy Ann and Andy banks, 11" tall, plastic, ©1972 Bobbs-Merrill Co. Inc., by My Toy Co., $18.00–22.00 set.

BOOKS

All of the books on pages 41–44 were written by Johnny Gruelle.

Left: *Raggedy Ann Stories,* ©1961 Bobbs-Merrill Co. Inc.; right: *Raggedy Andy Stories,* ©1960 Bobbs-Merrill Co.; Inc.; $15.00–20.00 each.

Left: *Raggedy Ann Stories,* ©1918 M.A. Donohue Co.; right: *Raggedy Andy Stories,* ©1920 M. A. Donohue Co.; $30.00–35.00 each.

Left: *Raggedy Ann Stories,* ©1918 P.F. Volland Co.; right: *Raggedy Andy Stories,* ©1920 P.F. Volland Co.; $75.00–85.00 each. Photo on right shows the back cover of books.

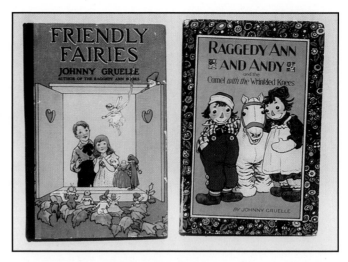

Left: ***Raggedy Ann Stories,*** ©1947 Bobbs-Merrill Co. Inc.; right: ***Raggedy Andy Stories,*** ©1948 Bobbs-Merrill Co. Inc.; $20.00–25.00 each.

Left: ***Friendly Fairies,*** ©1919 M.A. Donohue Co.; right: ***Camel with the Wrinkled Knees,*** ©1924 P.F. Volland Co.; $75.00–85.00 each.

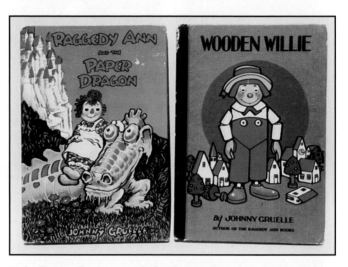

Left: ***Raggedy Ann's Wishing Pebble,*** ©1960 Bobbs-Merrill Co. Inc., $18.00–25.00. Right: ***Beloved Belindy,*** ©1926 P.F. Volland Co., $85.00–95.00.

Left: ***Raggedy Ann and the Paper Dragon,*** ©1972 Bobbs-Merrill Co. Inc., $18.00–25.00. Right: ***Wooden Willie,*** ©1954 M.A. Donohue Co., $30.00–35.00.

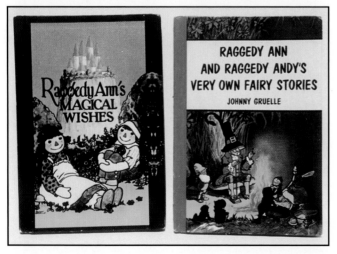

Left: ***Raggedy Ann's Magical Wishes,*** ©1928 M.A. Donohue Co., by Johnny Gruelle Co., $35.00–40.00. Right: ***Raggedy Ann and Andy's Very Own Fairy Stories,*** ©1960 Bobbs-Merrill Co. Inc., $20.00–25.00.

Left: ***Marcella,*** ©1929 M.A. Donohue Co., $75.00–85.00. Right: ***Raggedy Ann and the Deep Deep Woods,*** ©1960 Bobbs-Merrill Co. Inc., $20.00–25.00.

Left: ***Raggedy Ann in Cookie Land,*** ©1960 Bobbs-Merrill Co. Inc., $20.00–25.00. Right: ***Raggedy Ann's Lucky Pennies,*** ©1932 M.A. Donohue Co., by Johnny Gruelle Co., $35.00–40.00.

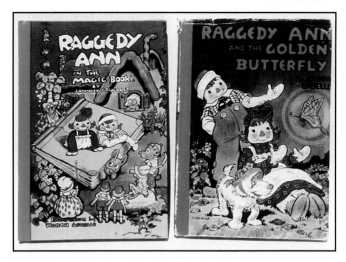

Left: ***Raggedy Ann in the Magic Book,*** ©1961 Bobbs-Merrill Co. Inc., $20.00–25.00. Right: ***Raggedy Ann and the Golden Butterfly,*** ©1940 Kingsport Press, $25.00–30.00.

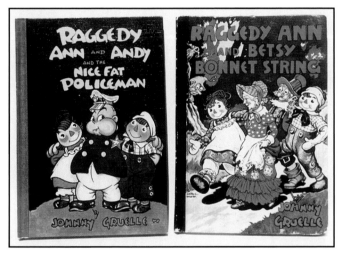

Left: ***Raggedy Ann and Andy and the Nice Fat Policeman,*** ©1960 Bobbs-Merrill Co. Inc.; right: ***Raggedy Ann and Betsy Bonnet String,*** ©1960 Bobbs-Merrill Co. Inc.; $20.00–25.00 each.

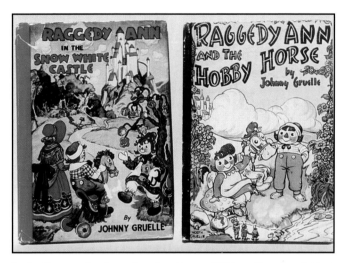

Left: ***Raggedy Ann in the Snow White Castle,*** ©1946 Johnny Gruelle Co, $30.00–35.00. Right: ***Raggedy Ann and the Hobby Horse,*** ©1961 Bobbs-Merrill Co. Inc., $20.00–25.00.

Left: ***Raggedy Ann and the Wonderful Witch,*** ©1961 Bobbs-Merrill Co. Inc.; right: ***Raggedy Ann and the Golden Ring,*** ©1961 Bobbs-Merrill Co. Inc.; $20.00–25.00 each.

Left: ***Raggedy Ann and the Happy Meadow,*** ©1961 Bobbs-Merrill Co. Inc., $20.00–25.00. Right: ***Raggedy Ann and Andy's Green Thumb Book,*** by Alix Nelson, illustrations by Johnny Gruelle, ©1975 Bobbs-Merrill Co. Inc., $40.00–45.00.

Left: ***More Raggedy Ann and Andy Stories,*** ©1977 Bobbs-Merrill Co. Inc.; right: ***Raggedy Ann and Andy's Animal Friends,*** ©1974 Bobbs-Merrill Co. Inc.; $20.00–25.00 each.

Left: ***Raggedy Ann and Andy and Witchie Kissabye,*** ©1975 Bobbs-Merrill Co. Inc.; right: ***Raggedy Ann and Andy's Sunny Stories,*** ©1974 Bobbs-Merrill Co. Inc.; $20.00–25.00 each.

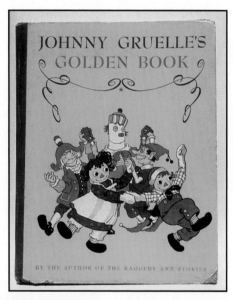

Johnny Gruelle's Golden Book, 12¼" x 9¾", 95 pages, hardcover, 1925 M. A. Donohue & Co., $85.00–95.00.

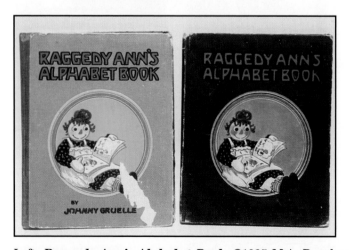

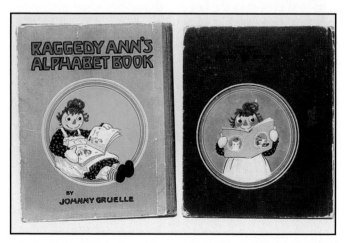

Left: ***Raggedy Ann's Alphabet Book,*** ©1925 M.A. Donohue Co., $40.00–45.00. Right: ***Raggedy Ann's Alphabet Book,*** ©1925 P.F. Volland Co., $45.00–50.00. Right photo shows the back covers of books.

 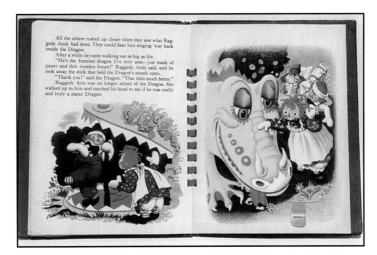

***Raggedy Ann and Andy* with Animated Illustrations,** animated by Julian Wher, pull tabs on pages and pictures move, ©1944 Saalfield Publishing Co., $55.00–65.00. Right photo shows inside of the book and its moving illustration tabs.

 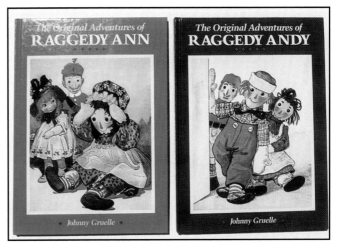

Left: ***Raggedy Ann, A Thank You, Please, and I Love You Book,*** ©1969 Bobbs-Merrill Co. Inc., by Golden Press; right: ***Raggedy Andy, The I Can Do It, You Can Do It Book,*** ©1973 Bobbs-Merrill Co. Inc., by Golden Press; $8.00–10.00 each.

Left: ***The Original Adventures of Raggedy Ann,*** ©1988 Macmillan Inc., by Derrydale Books; right: ***The Original Adventures of Raggedy Andy,*** ©1988 Macmillan Inc., by Derrydale Books; $10.00–12.00 each.

Left: ***Raggedy Ann and Andy Giant Treasury,*** by Johnny Gruelle, hardcover, ©1984 Bobbs-Merrill Co. Inc., by Derrydale books; right: ***Raggedy Ann and Andy Second Giant Treasury,*** by Johnny Gruelle, hardcover 11 x 8½", ©1989 Macmillan Inc., by Derrydale books; $20.00–25.00 each.

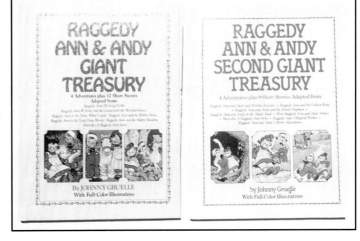

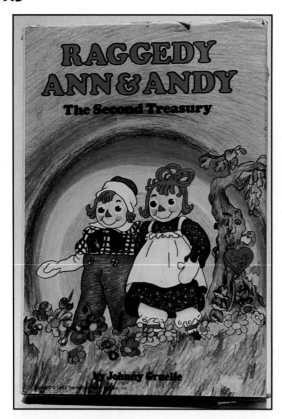

Raggedy Ann and Andy, The Second Treasury, ©1982 Bobbs-Merrill Co. Inc., by Lemon Tree Press, $20.00–25.00.

Raggedy Ann Stories to Read Aloud, by Johnny Gruelle, Wonder Book paperback, ©1960 by Johnny Gruelle Corp., $10.00–12.00.

Raggedy Ann and Andy's Cookbook, by Nika Hazelton, ©1975 Bobbs-Merrill Co. Inc., $20.00–25.00.

Raggedy Ann and Andy books, all are ©1992 Macmillan Inc., by Derrydale books, $8.00–12.00 each. Top left: *In the Playroom, A Pop-Up Book About Shapes.* Top right: *At the Park, A Pop-Up Book About Opposites.* Bottom left: *On the Farm, A Pop-Up Book About Animals.* Bottom right: *In the Garden, A Pop-Up Book About Numbers.*

Left: ***Raggedy Ann and the Daffy Taffy Pull, A Hallmark Pop-Up Book,*** ©1972 Bobbs-Merrill Co. Inc., by Hallmark; right: ***Adventures and Surprises with Raggedy Ann and Andy, A Hallmark Play-Time Book,*** has cardboard figures that can be moved throughout the storybook, ©1974 Bobbs-Merrill Co. Inc., by Hallmark; $25.00–30.00 each.

Wonder Books, all are $18.00–22.00 except where noted. Top left to right: ***Raggedy Ann and Marcella's First Day at School,*** ©1952 by the Johnny Gruelle Company; ***Raggedy Ann's Christmas Surprise,*** ©1952 by the Johnny Gruelle Company; ***A Puzzle for Raggedy Ann and Andy,*** ©1957 by the Johnny Gruelle Company. Bottom left to right: ***Raggedy Ann's Secret,*** ©1959 by the Johnny Gruelle Company; ***Raggedy Ann's Merriest Christmas,*** ©1952 by the Johnny Gruelle Company; ***Raggedy Ann's Tea Party,*** sculptured cover book, $15.00–18.00.

Whitman Tell-A-Tale books, $5.00–8.00 each. Top left to right: ***Raggedy Ann and the Tag Along Present,*** ©1971 Bobbs-Merrill Co. Inc.; ***Raggedy Andy's Treasure Hunt,*** ©1973 Bobbs-Merrill Co. Inc. Bottom left to right: ***Raggedy Ann's Cooking School,*** ©1974 Bobbs-Merrill Co. Inc.; ***Raggedy Ann and Andy on the Farm,*** ©1975 Bobbs-Merrill Co. Inc.; ***Raggedy Andy and the Jump-up Contest,*** ©1978 Bobbs-Merrill Co. Inc.

Little Golden Books, $8.00–10.00 each except where noted. Top left to right: ***Raggedy Ann and Fido,*** ©1969 Bobbs-Merrill Co. Inc., $12.00–15.00; ***Raggedy Ann and the Cookie Snatcher,*** ©1972 Bobbs-Merrill Co. Inc.; ***Raggedy Ann and Andy and the Rainy-Day Circus,*** ©1973 Bobbs-Merrill Co. Inc. Bottom left to right: ***Raggedy Ann and Andy The Little Gray Kitten,*** ©1975 Bobbs-Merrill Co. Inc.; ***Raggedy Ann and Andy Help Santa Claus,*** ©1977 Bobbs-Merrill Co. Inc.; ***Raggedy Ann and Andy Five Birthday Parties in a Row,*** ©1979 Bobbs-Merrill Co. Inc.

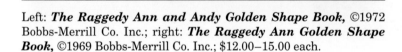

Left: ***The Raggedy Ann and Andy Golden Shape Book,*** ©1972 Bobbs-Merrill Co. Inc.; right: ***The Raggedy Ann Golden Shape Book,*** ©1969 Bobbs-Merrill Co. Inc.; $12.00–15.00 each.

Raggedy Ann's Favorite Things, A Golden Cloth Book, ©1972 Bobbs-Merrill Co. Inc., $15.00–18.00.

Soft cover books, 9" x 6½", ©1988 Macmillan Inc., by Random House. Top left: ***Raggedy Ann's Picture-Perfect Christmas;*** top right: ***Raggedy Ann and Andy's Department Store Caper;*** $8.00–10.00 each. **Soft cover books,** 5 x 5½", ©1987 Macmillan Inc., by Random House. Bottom left: ***Raggedy Ann at the Country Fair;*** bottom right: ***Raggedy Ann's Seashore Adventure;*** $5.00–8.00 each.

Left to right: ***This is Raggedy Ann,*** real cloth, by Whitman, $15.00–18.00; ***Play with Raggedy Andy,*** non-toxic, real cloth, wipes clean, ©1974 Bobbs-Merrill Co. Inc., by Whitman. $12.00–15.00; ***This is Raggedy Ann,*** non-toxic, real cloth, wipes clean. ©1970 Bobbs-Merrill Co. Inc. by Whitman, $12.00–15.00.

Left: ***Raggedy Ann at the Carnival,*** A Golden Look-Look Book, 8" x 8", ©1977 Bobbs-Merrill Co. Inc.; right: ***Raggedy Ann and Andy and the Magic Wishing Pebble,*** soft cover, 8" x 8", ©1987; $15.00–18.00 each.

Children's books, ©1980 Bobbs-Merrill Co. Inc., Weekly Reader Children's Book Club. Left: ***Raggedy Ann and Andy and the Pirates of Outgo Inlet;*** Right: ***Raggedy Ann and Andy in the Tunnel of Lost Toys;*** $15.00–18.00 each.

Left: ***Raggedy Ann and Andy Storybook,*** hardcover, ©1981 Bobbs-Merrill Co. Inc., by Johnny Gruelle, Grosset & Dunlap, $15.00–18.00. Right: ***Raggedy Ann and Andy Go Flying,*** A Golden Storytime Book, hardcover, ©1980 Bobbs-Merrill Co. Inc., $18.00–22.00.

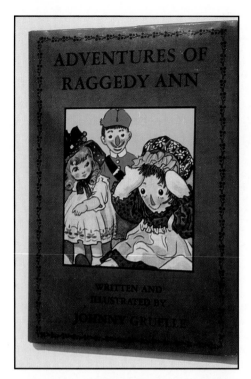

Left: ***Raggedy Ann I See You!,*** peek-a-board book, ©1987 Macmillan Inc., by Random House; right: ***Raggedy Ann's Book of Go-Togethers,*** hardboard pages and cover, ©1988 Macmillan Inc., by Random House; $8.00–10.00 each.

Adventures of Raggedy Ann, by Johnny Gruelle, 8 x 5½", hardcover, by Averel books, $12.00–15.00.

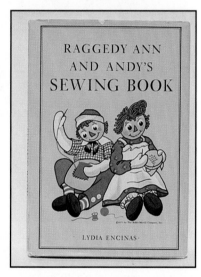

Raggedy Ann Gets Lost, hard board pages and cover, ©1987 Macmillan Inc., by Random House, $8.00–10.00.

Raggedy Ann and Andy's Sewing Book, ©1977 Bobbs-Merrill Co. Inc., by Lydia Encinas, $25.00–30.00.

Raggedy Ann Picture Book, real cloth, ©1947 by the Johnny Gruelle Co., by Saalfield Artcraft, $50.00–55.00.

Raggedy Ann and the Glad and Sad Day, A Golden Play And Learn Book, 13" tall, cardboard, ©1972 Bobbs-Merrill Co. Inc., $18.00–22.00.

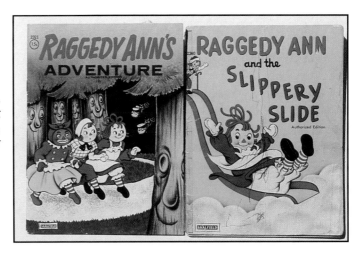

Left: ***Raggedy Ann's Adventure,*** soft cover, 8" x 6", ©1962 Bobbs-Merrill Co. Inc., by Saalfield Publishing Co.; right: ***Raggedy Ann and the Slippery Slide,*** soft cover, 8" x 6", ©1961 Bobbs-Merrill Co. Inc., by Saalfield Publishing Co.; $30.00–35.00 each.

Left: ***Raggedy Ann and the Laughing Brook;*** right: ***Raggedy Ann and the Hoppy Toad;*** both are ©1946 Perks Publishing, $35.00–40.00 each.

Left: ***Raggedy Ann and the Laughing Brook;*** right: ***Raggedy Ann and the Hoppy Toad;*** both are ©1944 by the American Crayon Company, $35.00–40.00 each.

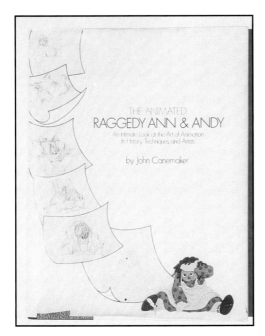

The Animated Raggedy Ann and Andy, hard cover, by John Canemaker, ©1977 Bobbs-Merrill Co. Inc., $25.00–30.00.

Raggedy Ann's Sweet and Dandy, Sugar Candy, Scratch and Sniff Book, hardcover, ©1976 Bobbs-Merrill Co. Inc., by Golden Press, $25.00–30.00.

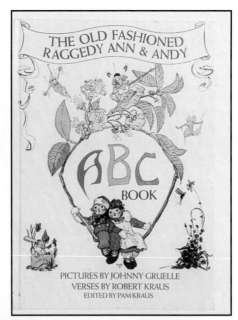

Left: ***Raggedy Ann's Nighttime Rescue,*** ©1987 Macmillan Inc., by Random House; right: ***The Old Fashioned Raggedy Ann and Andy ABC Book,*** hardcover, ©1981 Bobbs-Merrill Co. Inc., by Windmill Books Inc.; $12.00–15.00 each.

Left: ***The Original Adventures of Raggedy Ann and Raggedy Andy,*** hardcover, ©1991 Macmillan Inc., by Derrydale Books, $18.00–22.00. Right: ***Raggedy Ann and Andy Book,*** soft cover, 10" x 8", book is mostly written in Japanese, includes patterns to make various items, ©1992 by Phoenix Corporation LTD, $40.00–45.00.

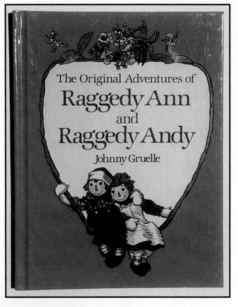

Raggedy Ann Sticker Book, 10½" x 12", ©1962 Bobbs-Merrill Co. Inc., Whitman book #1689:69, $25.00–30.00.

Raggedy Ann and Andy Color & Wipe-off Book, Things We Love, 12" tall, Golden book #1849-20, $15.00–18.00.

Raggedy Ann and Andy paper dolls, 13½" x 7", boxed set, ©1982 Bobbs-Merrill Co. Inc., by Whitman, $15.00–18.00.

Raggedy Ann Doll Book, 15½" x 7", ©1967 Bobbs-Merrill Co. Inc., by Whitman #1970, done by The Meyers, authorized edition; $15.00–18.00 each.

Raggedy Ann and Andy paper dolls, boxed set, ©1973 Bobbs-Merrill Co. Inc., by Whitman #4319/7209, $18.00–20.00.

Left: **Raggedy Ann and Andy paper dolls,** boxed set, ©1978 Bobbs-Merrill Co. Inc., by Whitman; right: **Raggedy Ann and Andy paperdolls,** boxed set, ©1975 Bobbs-Merrill Co. Inc., by Whitman, $18.00–20.00.

Left: ***Raggedy Ann and Andy A Paperdoll Book,*** ©1980 Bobbs-Merrill Co. Inc., Whitman book #1977-23; right: ***Raggedy Ann and Andy Fun Fashions for Paper Dolls,*** ©1974 Bobbs-Merrill Co. Inc., Whitman book #1962; $12.00–15.00 each.

Left: ***Raggedy Ann and Andy Circus Play Day, A Paper Doll Playbook,*** ©1980 Bobbs-Merrill Co. Inc., Whitman book #1838-31; right: ***Raggedy Ann and Andy Lollipop Fashions for Paper Dolls,*** ©1972 Bobbs-Merrill Co. Inc., Whitman book #1985; $15.00–18.00 each.

Left: ***Raggedy Ann and Andy Paper Dolls,*** ©1980 Bobbs-Merrill Co. Inc., Whitman book #1987-43; right: ***Raggedy Ann and Andy Circus Paper Dolls,*** ©1974 Bobbs-Merrill Co. Inc., Whitman book #1999; $12.00–15.00 each.

Left: ***Raggedy Ann Paper Doll,*** ©1970 Bobbs-Merrill Co. Inc., Whitman book #1970; right: ***Raggedy Ann and Andy Paper Dolls,*** ©1978 Bobbs-Merrill Co. Inc., Whitman book #1988-1; $12.00–15.00 each.

Left: ***Raggedy Ann and Andy Paper Dolls and Clothes,*** ©1966 Bobbs-Merrill Co. Inc., Whitman #1979, authorized edition by The Myers, $25.00–30.00. Right: ***Raggedy Ann and Andy A First Doll Book,*** "Flip a page, change an outfit," ©1969 Bobbs-Merrill Co. Inc., Whitman book #1970, authorized edition by The Myers, $18.00–22.00.

Raggedy Ann and Andy Paper Dolls, ©1961 Bobbs-Merrill Co. Inc., Saalfield #2739, authorized edition, $35.00–40.00.

Raggedy Ann and Andy Paper Dolls, ©1957 Johnny Gruelle Co., by Saalfield, authorized edition, #2754, $35.00–45.00.

Marcella's Raggedy Ann Doll Book, ©1940 Johnny Gruelle Co., by McLoughlin Bros Inc., $80.00–95.00.

Dell comic, *Raggedy Ann & Andy,* No. 452, ©1952 by the Johnny Gruelle Co., $25.00–30.00.

Dell comic, *Raggedy Ann and Andy*, Oct.–Dec. No. 1., ©1964 Bobbs-Merrill Co. Inc., $30.00–35.00.

Raggedy Ann and Andy Dell Junior Treasury comic, *The Camel with the Wrinkled Knees,* April 1957 No. 8, $25.00–30.00.

Raggedy Ann and Andy comic, "Higher and Higher — It's A Ride To Remember," ©1971 Bobbs-Merrill Co. Inc., Whitman No. 1, $20.00–25.00.

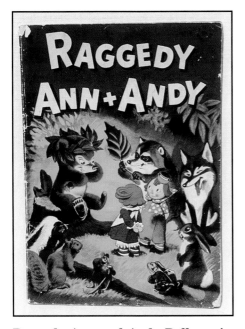

Raggedy Ann and Andy Dell comic,
July 1947, Vol I, No. 14, $30.00–35.00.

Raggedy Ann and Andy Dell comic,
July 1946, Vol I, No. 2. $30.00–35.00.

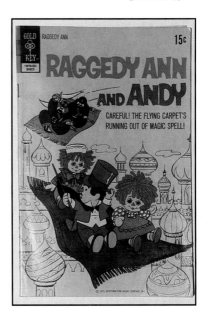

Raggedy Ann and Andy comic,
"Careful! The Flying Carpet's
Running Out of Magic Spell!,"
©1971 Bobbs-Merrill Co. Inc.,
No. 2 March 1972, by Western
Publishing Co., $18.00–22.00.

Left: *Raggedy Ann and Andy's Number Fun, A Coloring
Book,* ©1987 Macmillan Inc.; by Random House Inc.; right:
Raggedy Ann and Andy Stories to Color, ©1987 Macmillan
Inc., by Random House Inc.; $8.00–10.00 each.

Left: *Raggedy Ann's Coloring Book of
Opposites,* ©1987 Macmillan Inc., by Random
House Inc.; right: *Raggedy Ann and Andy in
the Playroom, A Coloring Book,* ©1987
Macmillan Inc., by Random House Inc.; $8.00–
10.00 each.

Raggedy Ann and Andy Dell comic,
Oct.–Dec., No. 3, ©1965 Bobbs-Merrill Co.
Inc., $28.00–32.00.

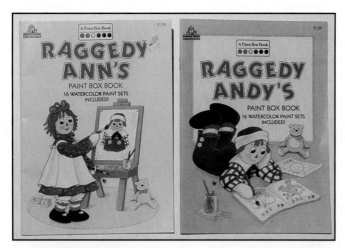

Left: ***Raggedy Ann's Paint Box Book,*** ©1987 Macmillan Inc., by Random House Inc.; right: ***Raggedy Andy's Paint Box Book,*** ©1987 Macmillan Inc., by Random House Inc.; $8.00–10.00 each.

Raggedy Ann's Trace 'n' Rub Coloring Book, ©1987 Macmillan Inc., by Random House Inc., $8.00–10.00.

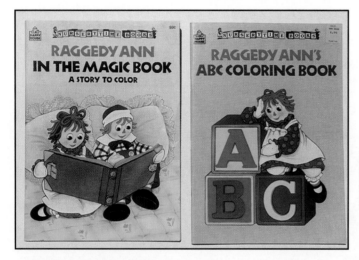

Left: ***Raggedy Ann in the Magic Book, A Story to Color,*** ©1987 Macmillan Inc., by Random House Inc.; right: ***Raggedy Ann's ABC Coloring Book,*** ©1987 Macmillan Inc., by Random House Inc.; $8.00–10.00 each.

Left: ***Raggedy Ann Coloring Book,*** ©1978 Bobbs-Merrill Co. Inc., Whitman book #1829-32; right: ***Raggedy Ann and Andy A Very Special Day Coloring Book,*** ©1979 Bobbs-Merrill Co. Inc., Whitman book #1660-35; $10.00–12.00 each.

Left: ***Raggedy Ann and Andy Coloring Book, An Airport Adventure,*** ©1978 Bobbs-Merrill Co. Inc., Whitman book #1053-42, $12.00–15.00. Right: **Coloring book, *Raggedy Ann and Andy with Raggedy Arthur,*** ©1980 Bobbs-Merrill Co. Inc., Whitman book #1654-32, $18.00–20.00.

Left: *Raggedy Ann Coloring Book,* ©1976 Bobbs-Merrill Co. Inc., Whitman book #1033-1; right: *Raggedy Ann Coloring Book with doll and clothes to Color and Cut Out,* ©1975 Bobbs-Merrill Co. Inc., Whitman book #1650; $12.00–15.00 each.

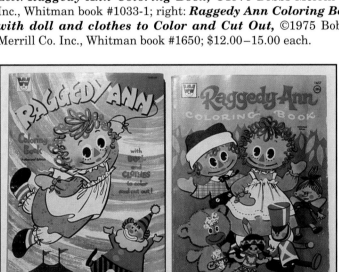

Raggedy Ann and Andy Coloring Book, ©1980 Bobbs-Merrill Co. Inc., Whitman book #1053-31, $10.00–12.00.

Left: *Raggedy Ann Coloring Book with Doll and clothes to color and cut out,* ©1971 Bobbs-Merrill Co. Inc., Whitman book #1657, $12.00–15.00. Right: *Raggedy Ann Coloring Book,* ©1972 Bobbs-Merrill Co. Inc., Whitman book #1657, $10.00–12.00.

Left: *Raggedy Ann Coloring Book,* ©1951 Johnny Gruelle Co., by Saalfield #1310-15, authorized edition, $35.00–40.00. Right: *Raggedy Ann and Andy Coloring Book,* ©1944 Johnny Gruelle Co., by Saalfield #2498, $45.00–55.00.

Left: ***Raggedy Ann and Andy Decorate a Tree with Love,*** ©1980 Bobbs-Merrill Co. Inc., Whitman book #2304-22, $18.00–22.00. Right: ***Raggedy Ann and Andy and the Santa Cookie Treat, A Paint with Water Book,*** ©1980 Bobbs-Merrill Co. Inc., Whitman book #2009-21, $10.00–12.00.

Raggedy Ann and Andy Coloring Book, ©1944 Johnny Gruelle Co., by Saalfield #370, $45.00–55.00.

Left: ***Raggedy Ann and Andy Dot to Dot,*** ©1978 Bobbs-Merrill Co. Inc., Whitman book #1289; right: ***Raggedy Ann, A Follow-the-Dot Book,*** ©1972 Bobbs-Merrill Co. Inc., Whitman book #1023; $12.00–15.00 each.

Raggedy Ann and Andy, An Activity Book, ©1982 Bobbs-Merrill Co. Inc., Whitman book #1148-1, $12.00–15.00.

Left: ***Raggedy Ann and Andy Learn to Count, A Sticker/Activity Book,*** ©1979 Bobbs-Merrill Co. Inc., Whitman book #1887, $10.00–12.00. Right: ***Raggedy Ann and Andy's Dandy Do-It Book!*** activity book, ©1978 Bobbs-Merrill Co. Inc., Golden Book, $15.00–18.00.

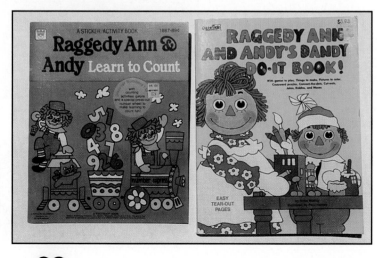

Left: ***Raggedy Ann Paint Book,*** ©1981, 1976 Bobbs-Merrill Co. Inc., Whitman book #1617-40, $12.00–15.00. Right: ***Raggedy Ann and Andy Sticker Fun "The Fortune Teller's Spell,"*** ©1980 Bobbs-Merrill Co. Inc., Whitman book #2195-31, $18.00–22.00.

Left: ***Raggedy Ann Has a Big Beautiful Birthday Party sticker fun,*** ©1972 Bobbs-Merrill Co. Inc., Whitman book #2173, $15.00–18.00. Right: ***Raggedy Ann Trace and Color***, ©1979 Bobbs-Merrill Co. Inc., Whitman book #1624, $10.00–12.00.

Raggedy Ann and Andy Hang-Ups, wall decorations, ©1972 Bobbs-Merrill Co. Inc., Whitman Book #1931, $15.00–18.00.

Left: ***Raggedy Ann Paint with Water***, ©1980 Bobbs-Merrill Co. Inc., Whitman book #1819; right: ***Raggedy Ann and Andy Paint with Water***, ©1982 Bobbs-Merrill Co. Inc., Whitman book #1818-33; $10.00–12.00 each.

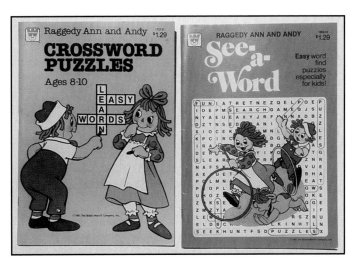

Left: ***Raggedy Ann and Andy Crossword Puzzles,*** ©1981 Bobbs-Merrill Co. Inc., Whitman book #1737-31; Right: ***Raggedy Ann and Andy See-a-Word,*** ©1981 Bobbs-Merrill Co. Inc., Whitman book #1809-44; $10.00–12.00 each.

CERAMICS

Raggedy Ann and Andy cookie jars, 9" ceramic jars made in Japan, $25.00–30.00 each.

Raggedy Ann and Andy cookie jars, 10" ceramic jars made by Napcoware of Japan, $30.00–35.00 each.

Raggedy Ann cookie jar, 11", ceramic, made by Twin Winton, $60.00–65.00.

Raggedy Ann cookie jar, 11", ceramic, made by McCoy, $95.00–105.00.

Raggedy Ann and Andy cookie jar, 10", glass, ©1977 Bobbs-Merrill Co. Inc., $70.00–75.00.

Raggedy Andy cookie jar, 10", ceramic, made in Japan, $30.00–35.00.

Raggedy Ann and Andy cookie jar, 9", tin with plastic lid, ©1973 Bobbs-Merrill Co. Inc., by Cheinco, $25.00–30.00.

Raggedy Ann creamer and Raggedy Andy sugar, 5½", ceramic, ©1993 Macmillan Inc., made in China, $30.00–35.00 each.

Raggedy Ann and Andy cookie jars, 13½" and 13¼" tall, ceramic, both are ©1993 Macmillan Inc. and made in Taiwan, $75.00–80.00 each.

Raggedy Ann and Andy salt and pepper shakers, 3¾", ceramic, ©1993 Macmillan Inc., made by Certified International Corp., #6604, $20.00–25.00 pair.

Raggedy Ann salt and pepper shakers, 3¾", ceramic, ©1993 Macmillan Inc., made by Certified International Corp., #6604, $20.00–25.00.

COLLECTIBLES

Raggedy Ann and Andy porcelain figurine on wooden base, 5" x 8", #4541 "OOPS" by Flambro, limited edition of 3,500, $50.00–65.00.

Raggedy Ann and Andy porcelain figurine on wooden base, 5" x 7", #4540 "Wet Paint" by Flambro, limited edition of 3,500, $50.00–65.00.

Raggedy Ann and Andy porcelain figurine on wooden base, 6" x 10", #4542 "Giddy Up" by Flambro, limited edition of 3,500, $75.00–85.00.

Raggedy Ann and Andy porcelain figurine on wooden base, 5" x 8", #4543 "70 Years Young" by Flambro, limited edition of 2,500, $85.00–95.00.

Raggedy Ann porcelain figurines, by Flambro, 6" tall. Left to right: #4510A, #4510B, #4510C; $15.00–18.00 each.

Raggedy Andy porcelain figurines, by Flambro, 6" tall. Left to right: #4520A, #4520B, #4520C; $15.00–18.00 each.

Raggedy Ann and Andy porcelain figurines, by Flambro, 4½" tall, ©1990, $8.00–10.00 each.

Raggedy Ann and Andy porcelain figurines, by Flambro, 4½" tall, ©1990, $8.00–10.00 each.

Raggedy Ann and Andy porcelain plaque, 3¾" x 4", "Raggedy Ann and Andy collectibles sold here," by Flambro, ©1987 Macmillan Inc., $20.00–$25.00.

Raggedy Ann and Andy porcelain bookends, by Flambro (Ann #4557, Andy #4556), ©1990 Macmillan Inc., $50.00–60.00 for pair

Raggedy Ann and Andy Christmas ornaments, 4¼", porcelain figurines by Flambro, ©1989, $10.00–12.00 each.

Raggedy Ann and Andy porcelain plate, 8½" diameter, limited edition of 10,000, by Flambro, ©1987 Macmillan Inc., $30.00–35.00.

Raggedy Ann and Andy collectible porcelain figurines, 8½", #4573, ©1990 by Flambro, $35.00–40.00 set.

Raggedy Ann cel from *The Adventures of Raggedy Ann and Andy,* 12" x 15", ©CBS Inc, from episode #13 "The Magic Wings Adventure," one of one, ©1990 Macmillan Inc., $125.00–150.00.

Raggedy Ann and Andy cel, 24" x 30", two original cels and two original drawings all from *The Adventures of Raggedy Ann and Andy,* ©CBS Inc, from episodes #10 "Sacred Cat Adventure" and #5 "Pixling Adventure," one of one, ©1990 Macmillan Inc., $400.00–500.00. On right, close-up of Raggedy Andy panel.

Left: **Raggedy Ann Christmas 1978 glass ball ornament,** third limited edition; right: **"Snowtime Frolic" Christmas 1981 glass ball ornament,** sixth limited edition; both are ©Bobbs-Merrill Co. Inc. and made by Schmid; $12.00–15.00 each.

Left: **Raggedy Ann Christmas 1980 glass ball ornament,** fifth limited edition; right: **Raggedy Ann Christmas 1983 glass ball ornament,** eighth limited edition; both are ©Bobbs-Merrill Co. Inc. and made by Schmid; $12.00–15.00 each.

Christmas 1980 figurine ornament, "First Run," first limited edition, ©Bobbs-Merrill Co. Inc., by Schmid, $20.00–25.00.

Left: **Christmas 1977 porcelain bell,** second limited edition; right: **Mother's Day 1978 porcelain bell,** third limited edition; both ©Bobbs-Merrill Co. Inc. and made by Schmid; $20.00–25.00 each.

Left: **1976 Mother's Day plate,** ceramic, first limited edition; right: **1977 Mother's Day plate,** ceramic, second limited edition; both are ©Bobbs-Merrill Co. Inc. and made by Schmid; $12.00–15.00 each.

Left: **1978 Mother's Day plate,** ceramic, third limited edition; right: **1979 Mother's Day plate,** ceramic, fourth limited edition of 10,000, sequentially numbered; both are ©Bobbs-Merrill Co. Inc. and made by Schmid; $12.00–15.00 each.

Left: **1975 Christmas plate,** ceramic, first limited edition; right: **1976 Christmas plate,** ceramic, second limited edition; both ©Bobbs-Merrill Co. Inc. and made by Schmid; $12.00–15.00 each.

Left: **1977 Christmas plate,** ceramic, third limited edition; right: **1978 Christmas plate,** ceramic, fourth limited edition; both ©Bobbs-Merrill Co. Inc. and made by Schmid; $12.00–15.00 each.

Left: **1979 Christmas plate,** ceramic, fifth limited edition of 15,000 sequentially numbered, $12.00–15.00. Right: **1976 Bicentennial plate,** ceramic, limited edition, $20.00–25.00. Both are ©Bobbs-Merrill Co. Inc. and made by Schmid.

Left: **1978 Valentine Day plate,** ceramic, first limited edition; right: **1979 Valentine Day plate,** ceramic, second limited edition; both are ©Bobbs-Merrill Co. Inc. and made by Schmid; $12.00–15.00 each.

Left: **1980 annual plate,** "The Sunshine Wagon," ceramic, first edition; right: **1981 annual plate,** "Raggedy Shuffle," ceramic, second edition; each plate limited to 10,000, sequentially numbered; both are ©Bobbs-Merrill Co. Inc. and made by Schmid; $25.00–30.00 each.

1982 annual plate, "Flying High," ceramic, third edition limited to 10,000, sequentially numbered, ©Bobbs-Merrill Co. Inc., made by Schmid, $25.00–30.00.

1984 annual plate, "Rocking Rodeo," ceramic, fifth and final edition limited to 10,000, sequentially numbered, ©Bobbs-Merrill Co. Inc., made by Schmid, $25.00–30.00.

COLORFORMS® & PLAYSETS

Raggedy Ann and Andy Super Deluxe Playhouse, 15½" x 12", Colorforms, ©1988 Macmillan Inc., $8.00–12.00.

Raggedy Ann Pop-up Tea Party, 12½" x 16", © Bobbs-Merrill Co. Inc., Colorforms Activity Toy, $25.00–30.00.

Raggedy Ann and Andy Pre-school Play Set, 12½" x 16", by Colorforms, ©1980 Bobbs-Merrill Co. Inc., $18.00–22.00. Photo on the right shows inside of play set.

Raggedy Ann and Andy Doll House, A Colorforms Activity Toy, 12½" x 16", ©1974 Bobbs-Merrill Co. Inc., $18.00–22.00.

Raggedy Ann and Andy Adventure Playset, "Presto Magix…colorful plastic stick-ons that stick n' lift like magic," Rose Art Brand #1805, 1993 Macmillan Inc., $5.00–8.00.

Raggedy Ann and Andy Acrylic Paint by Number Set, two 8" x 10" panels, by Craftmaster #16890, 1977 Bobbs-Merrill Co. Inc., $10.00–15.00.

Raggedy Ann and Andy Shrinky Dinks, kit #8100, 1976 Bobbs-Merrill Co. Inc., $15.00–20.00.

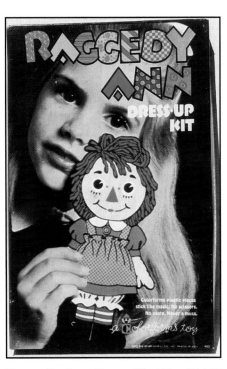

Raggedy Ann and Andy Colorforms Play Pak, 9" x 6", ©1988 Macmillan Inc., $12.00–15.00.

Raggedy Ann Dress-Up Kit, ©1967 Bobbs-Merrill Co. Inc., by Colorforms, $20.00–25.00.

Raggedy Ann Colorforms Dress-Up Set, ©1988 Macmillan Inc., $10.00–14.00.

Raggedy Ann Play Kitchen, by Colorforms, ©1975 Bobbs-Merrill Co. Inc., $18.00–22.00.

Raggedy Ann Sewing Cards, six cards to sew, ©1988 Macmillan Inc., by Colorforms, $10.00–12.00.

Raggedy Andy Sew and Love, by Colorforms, ©1975 Bobbs-Merrill Co. Inc., $22.00–25.00.

Raggedy Ann easy needlepoint, by Colorforms, ©1990 Macmillan Inc., $15.00–18.00.

Raggedy Ann sew-ons, lace and dress dolls, by Colorforms, ©1974 Bobbs-Merrill Co. Inc., $18.00–22.00.

Raggedy Ann sew-ons, lace and dress dolls, by Colorforms, ©1976 Bobbs-Merrill Co. Inc., $18.00–22.00.

Raggedy Ann Surprise Package, eight various activities, by Colorforms, ©1975 Bobbs-Merrill Co. Inc., $18.00−22.00.

Raggedy Ann 8 Great Activities, eight various activities, by Colorforms, ©1976 Bobbs-Merrill Co. Inc., $18.00−22.00.

"Raggedy Ann and Andy" Paste and Stick, by Whitman, boxed set includes paste and crayons, ©1968 Bobbs-Merrill Co. Inc., $25.00−30.00.

Raggedy Ann and Andy Paint By Number Set, item #4500, Art Award Co., 1988 Macmillan Inc., $5.00−8.00.

DOLLS

16" Raggedy Ann, made by P.F. Volland Co, circa 1930s, has wooden heart in chest under cloth, rare face type, has only one eyelash under eye, $1,500.00 and up. Above is a close-up photo of doll's face.

15" Raggedy Andy, made by American Toy and Novelty Mfg. Co. Inc., circa 1940s, has oil cloth face, $145.00–175.00. Above is a close-up photo of doll's face.

12½" Awake/Asleep Raggedy Ann, made by Georgene Novelties Co. Inc. in USA, circa 1940–1945, photos show both sides of doll, $275.00–325.00.

12½" Awake/Asleep Raggedy Andy, made by Georgene Novelties Co. Inc. in USA, circa 1940–1945, photos show both sides of doll, $275.00–325.00.

13" Awake/Asleep Raggedy Andy, made by Georgene Novelties Co. Inc. in USA, circa late 1930s to 1940, has black outline around nose, $300.00–325.00.

13" Awake/Asleep Raggedy Andy, made by Georgene Novelties Co. Inc. in USA, circa late 1930s to 1940, has black outline nose, $225.00–250.00 in this condition.

19" Raggedy Andy with black outline nose, made by Georgene Novelties Co. Inc. in USA, circa 1938–1945, $325.00–350.00.

19" Raggedy Andy with black outline nose, made by Georgene Novelties Co. Inc. in USA, circa 1938–1945, $325.00–350.00.

19" Raggedy Ann and Andy with black outline nose, both made by Georgene Novelties Co. Inc, in USA. Raggedy Ann is circa 1938–1945, $325.00–350.00. Raggedy Andy is one of the first produced by Georgene, circa 1938–1940, $375.00–400.00.

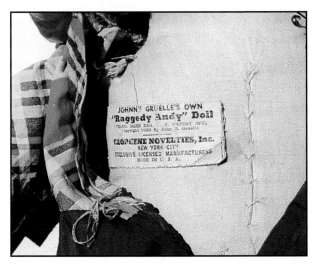

This shows the body tag from the above Raggedy Andy. Body tags were printed in blue for Raggedy Andy and red for Raggedy Ann. These tags were on the first Georgenes produced. Very hard to find.

15" Raggedy Ann dolls, made by Georgene Novelties Co. Inc. in USA, 1946–1963, note the same dress pattern done in different colors, $80.00–95.00 each.

15" Raggedy Ann and Andy pair, made by Georgene Novelties Co. Inc. in USA, 1946–1963, $80.00–95.00 each.

15" Raggedy Ann and Andy pair, made by Georgene Novelties Co. Inc. in USA, 1946–1963, unusual dress and shirt pattern, $85.00–105.00 each.

15" Raggedy Ann and Andy pair, made by Georgene Novelties Co. Inc. in USA, 1946–1963, $80.00–95.00 each.

15" Raggedy Ann and Andy pair, made by Georgene Novelties Co. Inc. in USA; Ann is dressed in Knickerbocker doll clothing; Andy shows wear on hair; $60.00–75.00 each.

15" Raggedy Anns, made by Georgene Novelties Co. Inc. in USA, 1946–1963, $80.00–95.00 each.

15" Raggedy Ann, made by Georgene Novelties Co. Inc. in USA, 1945–1946, 1963, $35.00–45.00 due to facial soil.

15" Raggedy Ann and Andy pair, made by Georgene Novelties Co. Inc. in USA, late 1950s to 1963, $75.00–85.00.

15" Raggedy Anns and Andy, made by Georgene Novelties Co. Inc. in USA, late 1950s to 1963, $45.00 for nude dolls, $65.00 for dressed Andy.

15" Raggedy Anns, made by Georgene Novelties Co. Inc. in USA, 1946–1963, doll on left is re-dressed, $55.00–75.00 each depending on clothing and condition.

15" **Raggedy Ann and Andy pair,** made by Georgene Novelties Co., Inc. in USA, 1946–1963, in original box, $165.00–180.00 each. Above right photo is the end cap of a Georgene doll box.

15" **Raggedy Ann and Andy pair,** made by Georgene Novelties Co. Inc. in USA, 1950s–1963, Andy has original paper tag, $95.00–125.00 each.

19" **Raggedy Andy,** made by Georgene Novelties Co. Inc. in USA, $105.00–125.00.

19" **Raggedy Andys,** made by Georgene Novelties Co. Inc. in USA, 1946–1963, $95.00–125.00 each.

19" **Raggedy Anns,** made by Georgene Novelties Co. Inc. in USA, 1946–1963, $95.00–125.00 each.

19" **Raggedy Ann and Andy pair,** made by Georgene Novelties Co. Inc. in USA, 1946–1963, $95.00–125.00 each.

19" **Raggedy Ann and Andy pair,** made by Georgene Novelties Co. Inc. in USA, 1946–1963, $95.00–125.00 each.

19" **Raggedy Ann,** made by Georgene Novelties Co. Inc. in USA, 1946–1963, $95.00–125.00.

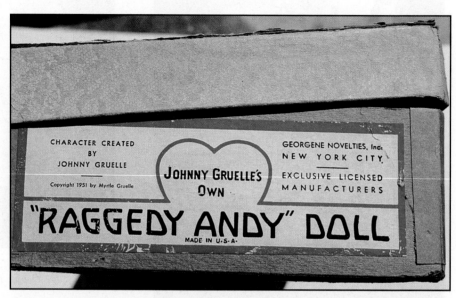

19" Raggedy Andy, made by Georgene Novelties Co., Inc. in USA, 1946–1963, shown in original box with paper tag, $225.00–250.00. End cap of Georgene doll box shown above.

Close-up of dolls shown.

19" Raggedy Ann, made by Georgene Novelties Co. Inc. in USA, 1946–1963, $125.00–150.00.

22" Raggedy Anns, made by Georgene Novelties Co. Inc. in USA, 1946–1963, $125.00–145.00 each.

22" Raggedy Ann, made by Georgene Novelties Co. Inc. in USA, 1946–1963, $125.00–145.00

22" Raggedy Andy, made by Georgene Novelties Co. Inc. in USA, 1946–1963, $125.00–145.00.

22" Raggedy Ann, made by Georgene Novelties Co. Inc. in USA, 1946–1963, $125.00–145.00.

22" Raggedy Ann, made by Georgene Novelties Co. Inc. in USA, circa 1945–1948, notice her feet are made with same material as her dress, $225.00–250.00.

30" Raggedy Andy, made by Georgene Novelties Co. Inc. in USA, early to mid-1940s, very unusual multicolored striped legs, $375.00–450.00.

30" Raggedy Ann and Andy pair, made by Georgene Novelties Co. Inc. in USA, early to mid 1940s, $350.00–375.00 each. Close-up photo of dolls shown above.

Close-up photo of a 30" Raggedy Ann, made by Georgene Novelties Co. Inc. in USA, replaced dress, unusual because of her five eyelashes instead of the typical four, $155.00–175.00.

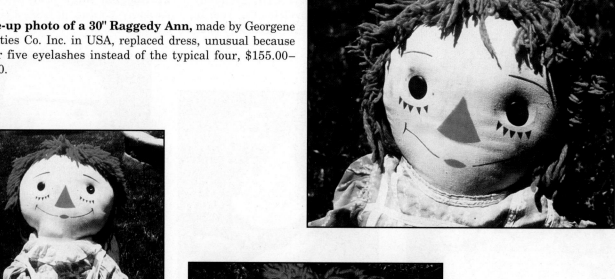

50" Raggedy Ann, made by Georgene Novelties Co. Inc. in USA, extremely unusual size, has no heart or tag, note close-up of face, $575.00–650.00.

30" Raggedy Ann and Andy, both made by Georgene Novelties Co. Inc. in USA, 1946–1963, $250.00–275.00 each.

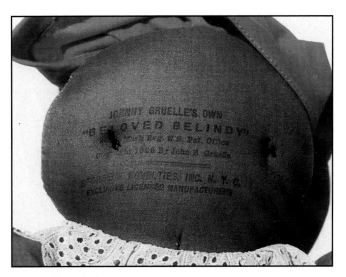

Left: **Beloved Belindy,** made by Georgene Novelties Co. Inc. in USA, 1938–1950, $950.00–1,250.00. Above: Close-up of stamp found on back of Beloved Belindy's head.

19" Raggedy Ann and Andy, made by Reliable Toy Co. LTD in Canada, $175.00–195.00 each.

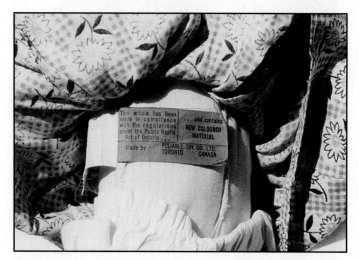 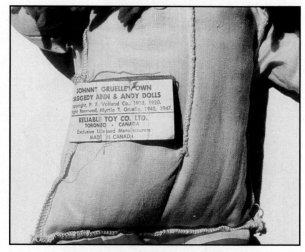

Body tags found on Reliable Toy Co. dolls shown in photos above. All body seams are stitched on the outside, unlike Georgene dolls which have body seams stitched on the inside. Since they look so similar to a Georgene doll, the seams would help identify a doll that no longer has its body tags.

5" Raggedy Ann and Andy miniature rag dolls, ©1976 Knickerbocker Toy Co. Inc., made in Taiwan, $15.00–18.00 each.

6" Raggedy Ann and Andy pair, Knickerbocker Toy Co. Inc., made in Taiwan, $10.00–12.00 each.

Raggedy Ann and Andy mini dolls, 3½" vinyl dolls, ©1973 Bobbs-Merrill Co. Inc., by Knickerbocker Toy Co. Inc, No. 9628, original box, $25.00–30.00.

Raggedy Ann and Andy Embraceables, 7" tall, original box, Knickerbocker Toy Co. Inc., #9216, ©1973, made in Taiwan, $25.00–30.00.

6" Raggedy Ann, Knickerbocker Toy Co., Inc, made in Taiwan, $10.00–15.00.

9" Raggedy Ann and Andy bean bag dolls, by Knickerbocker Toy Co., Inc., made in Taiwan, $10.00–15.00 each.

12" Raggedy Ann and Andy, by Knickerbocker Toy Co. Inc., made in Taiwan, $12.00–16.00 each.

12" Raggedy Andy and Ann marionettes, by Knickerbocker Toy Co., Inc., made in Taiwan, $40.00–45.00 each; in original box (on right), $65.00–75.00.

12" Raggedy Ann and Andy musical dolls, by Knickerbocker Toy Co., Inc., made in Taiwan, $20.00–25.00; with paper tag, $35.00.

Left: **15" Raggedy Andy,** by Knickerbocker Toy Co., Inc., made in Hong Kong; although doll is in near mint condition, its eyes have fallen out; $10.00–15.00 without eyes. Right: **15" Raggedy Ann,** by Knickerbocker Toy Co., Inc., made in Taiwan, has paper hang tag, late 1960s to early 1970s, $20.00–25.00.

15" Raggedy Anns, by Knickerbocker Toy Co., Inc., no tags, probably made in Korea, early to mid 1970s, $20.00–25.00 each.

15" Raggedy Anns, by Knickerbocker Toy Co., Inc., doll on left was made in Hong Kong; two others made in Taiwan, $15.00–25.00 each.

Left: **15" Raggedy Anns,** by Knickerbocker Toy Co., Inc., no tags but strange coloring and facial features, $20.00–25.00 each. Above: Close-up of dolls shows facial variations and coloring.

15" Raggedy Ann and Andy, by Knickerbocker Toy Co., Inc., Andy made in Hong Kong, Ann in New York; notice Ann has very thin leg stripes and eyes have been replaced, giving her a very unusual look; $25.00–30.00 each.

15" Raggedy Ann and Andy, early dolls by Knickerbocker Toy Co., Inc., made in New York, mid 1960s, $35.00–40.00 each.

15" Raggedy Ann and Andy, by Knickerbocker Toy Co., Inc., no tags but probably made in Hong Kong, unusual dress on Ann, $30.00–35.00 each.

15" musical Raggedy Anns, by Knickerbocker Toy Co., Inc.; doll on left plays "Rock-a-bye Baby" and was made in Hong Kong; doll on right plays "Pop Goes the Weasel" and was made in Taiwan; $35.00–40.00 each.

15" Raggedy Anns, early dolls by Knickerbocker Toy Co., Inc., made in Japan, orange wig variation is hard to find, $45.00–55.00 each.

15" Raggedy Ann and Andy, early dolls by Knickerbocker Toy Co., Inc., made in Japan, unusual dress for Ann, $45.00–55.00 each.

Close-up of the four early Raggedy Ann dolls made in Japan showing slight wig and facial variations. All have same hard-to-find dress pattern, but each is in a different color.

15" Raggedy Anns, early dolls by Knickerbocker Toy Co., Inc., made in Japan, both in excellent condition, $55.00–65.00 each.

15" Raggedy Ann and Andy, by Knickerbocker Toy Co., Inc., made in Hong Kong, unusual dark blushed cheeks, $30.00–35.00 each. On right is a close-up of Raggedy Ann's face.

15" Raggedy Ann and Andy, by Knickerbocker Toy Co., Inc., made in Malaysia, early to mid 1970s, $25.00–30.00 each.

15" Raggedy Ann and Andy, by Knickerbocker Toy Co., Inc., made in Taiwan, circa 1976–1978, $25.00–30.00 each.

15" Raggedy Ann and Andy, by Knickerbocker Toy Co., Inc., made in Taiwan, hard-to-find dress and matching apron on Ann, Andy wears very unusual aqua outfit, $40.00–45.00 each.

15" Raggedy Ann and Andy, by Knickerbocker Toy Co., Inc., made in Hong Kong, $35.00–40.00 each.

15" Raggedy Ann and Andy, by Knickerbocker Toy Co., Inc., made in Hong Kong; Andy is musical and plays "Rock-a-bye Baby"; $30.00–35.00 for Ann; $45.00–55.00 for Andy.

15" Raggedy Ann and Andy, by Knickerbocker Toy Co., Inc., made in Malaysia, $25.00–30.00 each.

15" Raggedy Ann and Andy, Ann has paper hang tag, by Knickerbocker Toy Co., Inc., made in Hong Kong, $30.00–35.00 each; $45.00 with hang tag.

15" Raggedy Ann and Andy, by Knickerbocker Toy Co., Inc., made in Taiwan, $20.00–25.00 for Ann; $30.00–35.00 Andy with hang tag.

15" Raggedy Ann and Andy, by Knickerbocker Toy Co., Inc., made in Taiwan, flat-faced look, very bushy hair, $25.00–30.00 each.

15" musical Raggedy Ann and Andy, by Knickerbocker Toy Co., Inc., made in Hong Kong, both play "Rock-a-bye Baby," $45.00–55.00 each.

15" Raggedy Ann and Andy, by Knickerbocker Toy Co., Inc., made in Hong Kong, Ann has unusual dress variation, $35.00–45.00 each.

15" Raggedy Ann and Andy, by Knickerbocker Toy Co., Inc., made in Taiwan, $20.00–25.00 each.

Left: **15" Raggedy Andys,** by Knickerbocker Toy Co., Inc., two strange variations. Andy on left has extremely unusual blue/white striped legs, appears to be original, no visual sign of tampering, $25.00–30.00. Andy on right has no hair, made in Taiwan, back of head is extremely unusual, $40.00–45.00. Right: Photo shows backside close-up of Raggedy Andy's head.

15" Raggedy Ann and Andy, by Knickerbocker Toy Co., Inc., tags read made in Taiwan, although they are early dolls, $35.00–40.00 each.

15" Raggedy Ann and Andy, by Knickerbocker Toy Co., Inc., made in Korea, $20.00–25.00 each.

15" Bedtime Raggedy Ann and Andy, by Knickerbocker Toy Co., Inc., made in Taiwan; dolls in left photo have plastic eyes; in right photo, iron-on eyes; $20.00–25.00 each.

15" Raggedy Anns and Andy, by Knickerbocker Toy Co., Inc., dolls on left and right were made in New York; doll in center made in Hong Kong; $30.00–40.00 each.

Left: **Box for 15" Raggedy Ann,** Knickerbocker Toy Co., Inc., ©1964 by Myrtle Gruelle, made in U.S.A., $25.00–30.00 for empty box. Above: Manufacturing information on side of box.

15" musical Raggedy Ann doll in original box, by Knickerbocker Toy Co., Inc., made in Taiwan, $85.00–95.00.

15" Raggedy Andy in original box, by Knickerbocker Toy Co., Inc., made in Hong Kong, $75.00–80.00.

15" Raggedy Ann and Andy pair in original box, by Knickerbocker Toy Co., Inc., made in Taiwan, $65.00–75.00 each.

15" Raggedy Ann and Andy pair in original box, by Knickerbocker Toy Co., Inc., made in Taiwan, $65.00–75.00 each.

15" Raggedy Andy in original box, by Knickerbocker Toy Co., Inc., made in Malaysia, $65.00–75.00.

15" Raggedy Ann and Andy pair in original box, by Knickerbocker Toy Co., Inc., made in Korea, $65.00–75.00 each.

15" Raggedy Andy in original box, by Knickerbocker Toy Co., Inc., made in Taiwan, ©1976, $65.00–75.00.

15" Raggedy Ann in original shipping box, by Knickerbocker Toy Co., Inc., made in Taiwan, probably a company promotional mail-in item, box postmarked 1971, $35.00–45.00.

15" Raggedy Andy in original shipping box, by Knickerbocker Toy Co., Inc., made in Taiwan, mailed from Procter and Gamble, box postmarked 1972, $35.00–45.00.

15" Raggedy Ann in original shipping box, by Knickerbocker Toy Co., Inc., made in Taiwan, mailed from Procter and Gamble, box postmarked 1972, $35.00–45.00.

19" Raggedy Ann and Andy pair, by Knickerbocker Toy Co., Inc., made in Taiwan, 1976–1978, $35.00–40.00 each.

19" Raggedy Ann and Andy pair, by Knickerbocker Toy Co., Inc., made in Taiwan, $30.00–35.00 each.

19" Raggedy Andy, by Knickerbocker Toy Co., Inc., made in Taiwan, unusual aqua blue outfit, $45.00–55.00.

Left: **19" Raggedy Ann and Andy pair,** early dolls by Knickerbocker Toy Co., Inc., made in Hong Kong, mid to late 1960's, $45.00–55.00. Above: Close-up of dolls' faces.

19" Raggedy Anns, by Knickerbocker Toy Co., Inc., made in Hong Kong, $45.00–55.00 each.

19" Raggedy Anns, by Knickerbocker Toy Co., Inc., all made in Taiwan, $25.00–30.00 each.

19" Raggedy Ann and Andy pair, by Knickerbocker Toy Co., Inc., made in Taiwan, late 1970s to early 1980s, $30.00–35.00 each.

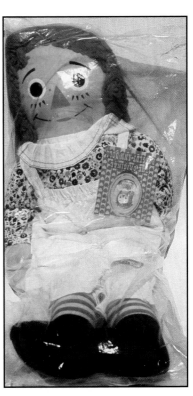

19" Raggedy Anns, by Knickerbocker Toy Co., Inc.; doll on left made in Taiwan; doll on right in Malaysia; $20.00–25.00 each.

19" Raggedy Ann in original box, by Knickerbocker Toy Co., Inc., made in Taiwan, ©1979, $65.00–75.00.

19" Raggedy Ann in original plastic baggie, Knickerbocker Toy Co., Inc., made in Taiwan, $45.00–50.00.

19" Raggedy Andy in original box, by Knickerbocker Toy Co., Inc., made in Taiwan, $85.00–95.00.

19" Raggedy Ann in original box, by Knickerbocker Toy Co., Inc., made in Taiwan, $85.00–95.00.

19" Raggedy Ann and Andy talking doll, pull-string talkers, by Knickerbocker Toy Co., Inc., made in Taiwan, $65.00–75.00 each.

20" Raggedy Ann Teach and Dress dolls, teaches child to buckle, button, lace, etc., by Knickerbocker Toy Co. Inc., made in Hong Kong, late 1960s; dolls have black eye dots and shiny black shoes; dress on right has more unusual pattern; $50.00–55.00 each.

20" Raggedy Ann and Andy Teach and Dress pair, earlier dolls with black eye dots, shiny black shoes, by Knickerbocker Toy Co. Inc., made in Hong Kong, $50.00–55.00 each.

20" Raggedy Ann and Andy Teach and Dress pair, by Knickerbocker Toy Co. Inc., made in Taiwan, early 1970s, both have red eye dots and dull black shoes, $45.00–50.00 each.

20" Raggedy Ann and Andy Teach and Dress pair, by Knickerbocker Toy Co. Inc., made in Taiwan, early 1970s, $45.00–50.00 each.

25" Raggedy Ann and Andy pair, by Knickerbocker Toy Co. Inc., made in Taiwan, circa 1976–1978, $55.00–65.00 each.

25" Raggedy Ann and Andy pair, by Knickerbocker Toy Co. Inc., made in Taiwan, $50.00–55.00 each.

25" Raggedy Ann and Andy pair, by Knickerbocker Toy Co. Inc., made in Malaysia, Ann has original paper tag, $65.00–75.00 each.

25" Raggedy Anns, by Knickerbocker Toy Co. Inc.; doll on left made in Hong Kong; doll on right in Taiwan, has desirable dress pattern; $75.00–95.00 each. Close-up shows difference in faces as well as the dress pattern.

25" Raggedy Anns, by Knickerbocker Toy Co. Inc. Doll on left made in Taiwan, $50.00–55.00. Doll on right made in New York, $75.00–95.00. Close-up shows difference in faces.

31" Raggedy Ann and Andy pair, by Knickerbocker Toy Co. Inc., made in Taiwan, $75.00–85.00 each.

31" Raggedy Ann and Andy pair, by Knickerbocker Toy Co. Inc., made in Hong Kong, $115.00–125.00 each.

31" Raggedy Ann and Andy pair, by Knickerbocker Toy Co. Inc., made in Taiwan, Andy has original paper tag, $85.00–95.00 each.

31" Raggedy Andy, by Knickerbocker Toy Co. Inc., made in Malaysia, has original paper tag, $115.00–125.00.

31" Raggedy Ann, by Knickerbocker Toy Co. Inc., made in Taiwan, $80.00–95.00.

31" Raggedy Andys, by Knickerbocker Toy Co. Inc. Doll on left made in Taiwan, $75.00–85.00. Doll on right made in New York, $115.00–125.00.

31" Raggedy Ann, by Knickerbocker Toy Co. Inc., made in Taiwan, has original paper tag, $115.00–125.00.

35" Raggedy Ann and Andy pair, by Knickerbocker Toy Co. Inc., sewn in China, dolls have original boxes shown below, $145.00–165.00 each with original box.

31½" Raggedy Ann doll in original box, by Knickerbocker Toy Co. Inc., made in Taiwan, $155.00–165.00.

Left: **38" Raggedy Ann and Andy musical dancing dolls,** by Knickerbocker Toy Co. Inc., made in Hong Kong, both have music boxes in their backs and elastic on feet so child can dance with them, very unusual dolls, Ann has hard-to-find hair color variation, $205.00–235.00 for Andy; $250.00–275.00 for Ann. Above: Close-up photo of Raggedy Ann shows her very rare hair color.

40" Raggedy Anns, by Knickerbocker Toy Co. Inc., made in Hong Kong, $125.00–145.00 each.

40" Raggedy Andy, by Knickerbocker Toy Co. Inc., made in Hong Kong, has original paper tag, $155.00–175.00 with paper tag.

40" Raggedy Ann, by Knickerbocker Toy Co. Inc., made in Hong Kong, very unusual dress pattern, $155.00–165.00.

40" Raggedy Ann and Andy, by Knickerbocker Toy Co. Inc., made in Taiwan, $125.00–135.00 each.

40" Raggedy Ann, by Knickerbocker Toy Co. Inc., made in Taiwan, $125.00–135.00.

45" Raggedy Ann and Andy dolls, by Knickerbocker Toy Co, Inc., made in Hong Kong, 45" dolls have five eyelashes instead of the standard four, $195.00–215.00 each.

38½" Raggedy Andy, by Knickerbocker Toy Co. Inc., made in Taiwan, has original paper tag and box (right), $165.00–185.00 with original paper tag and box.

45" Raggedy Ann and Andy, by Knickerbocker Toy Co. Inc., made in Taiwan, $150.00–175.00 each.

Beloved Belindy, by Knickerbocker Toy Co. Inc., made in Hong Kong, missing original outfit, $175.00–200.00.

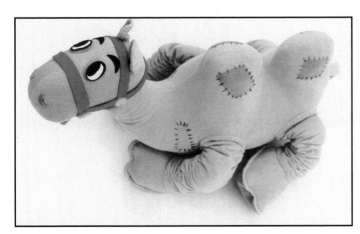

Camel with the Wrinkled Knees, 17" long, by Knickerbocker Toy Co. Inc., made in Taiwan, $195.00–225.00; camel with original box (lower left), $285.00–300.00.

Raggedy Arthur dog, by Knickerbocker Toy Co. Inc., made in Taiwan, $195.00–225.00.

5" Raggedy Ann and Andy babies, by Applause, $15.00–18.00 each.

7" Raggedy Ann and Andy musical dolls, head rotates when music plays, ©1986 Macmillan Inc., by Applause, $45.00–55.00 each.

8" Raggedy Ann and Andy sleeping bag dolls, by Applause, doll comes in their own sleeping bag, $15.00–18.00 each.

12" Raggedy Andy doll "Little Raggedys," ©Macmillan Inc., by Applause, $25.00–30.00.

12" Raggedy Ann and Andy Asleep/Awake dolls, by Applause, sleeping face on one side, awake on reverse, $25.00–30.00 each.

17" Raggedy Ann and Andy Sleepytime dolls, by Applause, $30.00–35.00 each.

15½" Raggedy Ann and Andy puppet dolls, ©1987 Macmillan Inc., by Applause, $45.00–50.00 each.

12" Raggedy Ann and Andy Valentine Dolls, ©Knickerbocker a division of Applause, note facial variation in photo on right, $40.00–45.00 each.

Left: **12" Raggedy Ann Christmas doll,** ©1981 Knickerbocker a division of Applause, $45.00–55.00. Right: **12" Raggedy Andy Doll,** ©1986 by Applause, $20.00–25.00.

12" Raggedy Ann and Andy pair, by Applause, $25.00–30.00 each.

12" Raggedy Ann and Andy pair, ©1981 Knickerbocker a division of Applause, original hang tags, $30.00–35.00 each.

20" original Raggedy Ann and Andy pair, by Applause, $45.00–55.00 each.

12" Raggedy Ann and Andy pair, ©1986 by Applause, $28.00–32.00 each.

12" Raggedy Ann and Andy pair, by Applause, $18.00–22.00 each.

16" Raggedy Ann and Andy pair, "classic" dolls, 70th Anniversary, ©1988 by Applause, $28.00–32.00 each.

36" Raggedy Ann and Andy pair, by Applause, $65.00–70.00 each.

25" Raggedy Andy, ©1986 by Applause, $45.00–50.00.

48" Raggedy Ann and Andy dancing doll pair, ©1986 Macmillan Inc., by Applause, elastic on feet and hands so that child can dance with doll, $115.00–125.00 each.

36" Raggedy Ann and Andy pair, ©1986 Applause, $75.00–80.00 each.

Left to right: **12" Raggedy Ann, 8" Raggedy Ann, and 12" Raggedy Ann,** all by Applause, shows facial variations, $8.00–12.00 each.

8" Raggedy Andys, all by Applause, shows facial variations, $8.00–12.00 each.

Left: **8" Raggedy Ann and Andy valentine dolls,** by Applause, $30.00–35.00. Right: **Raggedy Ann and Andy Gift Huggers store display box,** 6" x 16½", ©1988 Johnny Gruelle, by Applause, $75.00–80.00.

10" Camel with the wrinkled knees, ©1986, 1988 Macmillan Inc., by Applause, $65.00–75.00.

Left: **19" Raggedy Ann and Andy pair for 75th Anniversary,** first limited edition of 10,000, each piece is numbered, ©1992 Johnny Gruelle, by Applause, made to look like the early Georgene dolls, $125.00–135.00 set. Right: Boxes for the limited edition set.

19" Raggedy Ann and Andy, 2nd limited edition of 10,000, each piece is numbered, ©1993 Johnny Gruelle, by Applause, made to look like the Molly-E dolls, $55.00–60.00 each.

14" Baby Raggedy Ann, 2nd limited edition of 10,000, each piece is numbered, ©1993 Johnny Gruelle, by Applause, made to look like the Molly-E dolls, $45.00–50.00.

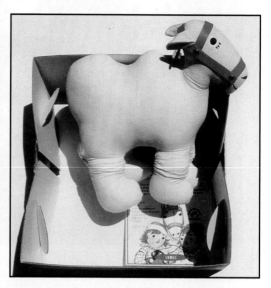

13" Raggedy Ann and Andy pair and 10½" Camel, 3rd limited edition of 10,000, each piece is numbered, ©1994 Johnny Gruelle by Applause, made to look like dolls in original Johnny Gruelle illustrations, $95.00–125.00 set.

Shows all the boxes for the 3rd limited edition set.

Raggedy Ann dolls, made by the Kusunoki Toy Co. LTD, Phoenix Corp LTD, very well made, manufactured and distributed in Japan only, no longer available. Left to right: 17½", $175.00–200.00; 23", $275.00–300.00; 29", $450.00–500.00.

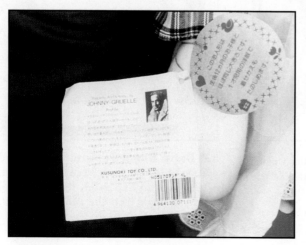

Close-up of paper hang tag from Kusunoki dolls, writing is in Japanese.

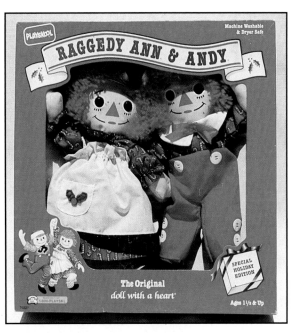

Raggedy Andy dolls, made by the Kusunoki Toy Co. LTD, Phoenix Corp LTD, very well made, manufactured and distributed in Japan only, no longer available. Left to right: 17½", $175.00–200.00; 23", $275.00–300.00; 29", $450.00–500.00.

12" Raggedy Ann and Andy Christmas dolls, ©1990 Playskool Inc., $35.00–40.00.

8½" Baby Raggedy Ann and Andy dolls, ©1989 Playskool, $10.00–14.00 each.

17" Raggedy Ann Christmas doll, ©1988 Playskool Inc., $35.00–40.00.

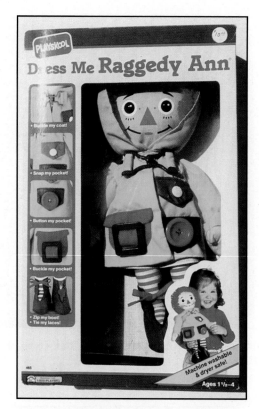

16" Dress Me Raggedy Ann doll, ©1991
Playskool, $20.00–25.00.

17" Heart-to-Heart Raggedy Ann doll,
battery operated, press your hand over her
heart and feel/hear her heartbeat, ©1992
Playskool Inc., $35.00–45.00.

8" Raggedy Ann and Andy pair, ©1992
Playskool Inc., $14.00–16.00 set.

9" Raggedy Ann and Andy dolls, cloth, ©1995
Kenner, Inc., $12.00–16.00 set.

21" Raggedy Anns, first official black Raggedy
Ann, ©1994 by Playskool, $20.00–25.00 for white
doll; $35.00–40.00 for black doll.

12" Little Raggedys Baby Dolls, ©1991 Macmillan Inc., by Direct Connect International Inc., $30.00–35.00 each.

12" Little Raggedys Nighty Night Dolls, ©1991 Macmillan Inc., by Direct Connect International Inc., $30.00–35.00 each.

6½" Little Raggedys Toy Toons, cloth bodies with rubber heads, ©1990 Macmillan Inc., by Direct Connect International Inc., $8.00–12.00 each.

7½" Raggedy Ann bean bag doll, cloth, ©1972 Bobbs-Merrill Co. Inc., made in Japan, $18.00–20.00.

Bean bag set: 8½" Ann, 8½" Andy, 8½" Belindy, and 6½" Camel; all by The Toy Works, ©1991 Macmillan Inc., $10.00–14.00 each.

9" Raggedy Ann and Andy "bend-em" dolls, cloth over wire, bendable, Knickerbocker Toy Co. Inc., Japan, late 1960s, $25.00–30.00 each.

11½" Raggedy Ann-type doll, has a rattle-type body that chimes when doll moves, by Dakin Dream Dolls "Merribelle #1251" prod. of Japan, $18.00–22.00.

Raggedy Ann and Andy clip-on dolls, cloth, 2½" set and 3½" set, ©1978 Bobbs-Merrill Co. Inc., $18.00–25.00 each set.

11" stuffed one-piece dolls, $35.00–40.00 each.

9" Raggedy Ann and Andy dolls, fully jointed plastic dolls, ©1975 Bobbs-Merrill Co. Inc., by Nasco Inc., $15.00–20.00 each.

18" Raggedy Andy doll, made of parachute-type material, by Department 56, $8.00–10.00.

24" Raggedy Ann and Andy dolls, plastic, ©1973 Bobbs-Merrill Co. Inc., by Nasco Doll Inc., $35.00–40.00 each.

30" Raggedy Ann ventriloquist doll, foam body, hard plastic head and arms, pull string in back to make mouth move, ©1973 Bobbs-Merrill Co. Inc., $85.00–95.00.

12" Raggedy Ann hand puppet, cloth with felt face and hands, no markings, probably late 1960s, $25.00–30.00.

6" Raggedy Ann and Andy dolls, ©Knickerbocker Toy Co. Inc., made for Hallmark Cards, $15.00–20.00 each.

Raggedy Ann and Andy doll and play set, ©1976 Bobbs-Merrill Co. Inc., by Knickerbocker Toy Co., $30.00–35.00 each.

6" Raggedy dolls, ©1974 Bobbs-Merrill Co. Inc., made for Hallmark, $20.00–25.00 each. Left to right: Raggedy Ann, Raggedy Andy, Beloved Belindy, Henny Penny, and Uncle Clem.

11" Raggedy Ann and Andy hand puppets, cloth with rubber heads, by Gund, ©1965 Bobbs-Merrill Co. Inc., $30.00–35.00 each.

10" Raggedy Ann and Andy hand puppets, cloth, ©1973 Knickerbocker Toy Co. Inc., made in Taiwan, $20.00–25.00 each.

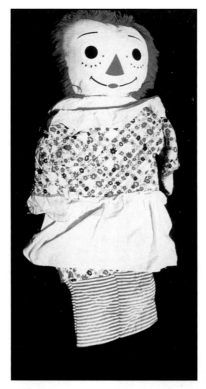

Raggedy Ann and Andy sleeping bags "dolls" for children, 52" long with side zipper, entrance at neck opening, head used as pillow, made by Knickerbocker Toy Co., $75.00–95.00 each.

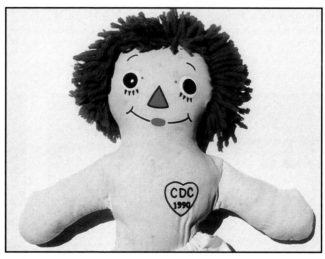

13" Awake/Asleep Raggedy Ann, limited number were handmade for the 1990 CDC convention (note marking found on doll), $75.00–95.00.

Left: **4¾" Raggedy Ann and Andy handmade dolls,** $10.00–12.00 pair. Right: **4¼" Raggedy Ann doll,** ©Knickerbocker Toy Co. Inc., for Hallmark, $12.00–15.00.

19" homemade Raggedy Ann and Andy pair, embroidered faces with appliqué noses, circa 1950s, $75.00–85.00 pair.

19" homemade Raggedy Ann and Andy, embroidered faces, appliqué noses, circa early 1940s, $150.00–175.00 each.

19" homemade Raggedy Ann and Andy pair, embroidered faces, black outline noses, circa 1950s, $95.00–105.00 pair.

Homemade dolls (left to right): **19" Raggedy Andy,** earlier doll with embroidered face, appliqué nose, multi-striped legs, outline nose, $75.00–80.00; **15" Awake/Asleep Raggedy Andy** with embroidered face, appliqué nose, circa 1950s, $55.00–$65.00; **15" Raggedy Ann** with painted face, made to look like an early doll but is probably circa 1980, $40.00–45.00; **15" Raggedy Andy** with embroidered face and appliqué nose, $35.00–45.00.

GAMES & TOYS

Raggedy Ann and Andy real woodboard puzzle, "Sharing A Swing," ©1987 Macmillan Inc., by Playskool, $12.00–15.00.

Raggedy Ann and Andy real woodboard puzzle, "A Gift for Someone Special," ©1987 Macmillan Inc., by Playskool, $12.00–15.00.

Raggedy Ann and Andy real woodboard puzzle, "Home Sweet Home," ©1987 Macmillan Inc., by Playskool, $12.00–15.00.

Raggedy Ann and Andy real woodboard puzzle, "Do the Raggedy Dance," ©1987 Macmillan Inc., by Playskool, $12.00–15.00.

Raggedy Ann and Andy frame tray puzzles, 14½" x 11", 25 pieces, ©1987 Macmillan Inc., by Milton Bradley, $10.00–12.00 each.

Raggedy Ann and Andy frame tray puzzles, 14½" x 11", 25 pieces, ©1988 Macmillan Inc., by Milton Bradley, $10.00–12.00 each.

Left: **Raggedy Ann and Andy frame tray puzzle,** 8" x 11½", ©1976 Bobbs-Merrill Co. Inc., by Whitman, $10.00–12.00. Right: **Raggedy Ann and Andy frame tray puzzle,** 8" x 11", by Golden, ©1978, 1984 Bobbs-Merrill Co. Inc., $10.00–12.00.

Left: **Raggedy Ann and Andy frame tray puzzle,** 8" x 11", ©1983 Bobbs-Merrill Co. Inc., by Golden, $10.00–12.00. Right: **Raggedy Ann and Andy frame tray puzzle,** 8" x 11", ©1978, 1984 Bobbs-Merrill Co. Inc., by Golden, $10.00–12.00.

Left: **Raggedy Ann and Andy frame tray puzzle,** 8" x 11", ©1976 Bobbs-Merrill Co. Inc., by Whitman, $10.00–12.00. Right: **Raggedy Ann and Andy frame tray puzzle,** 8" x 11", ©1980 Bobbs-Merrill Co. Inc., by Whitman, $10.00–12.00.

Raggedy Ann frame tray puzzle, 10" x 14", 20 pieces, ©1955 by the Johnny Gruelle Co., by Milton Bradley, $25.00–35.00.

Raggedy Ann and Andy jigsaw puzzles, 11½" x 16¼", over 100 pieces, ©1993 Macmillan Inc., by Rose Art; on left, "Camel Ride"; on right, "True Friends"; $10.00–12.00 each.

Raggedy Ann elementary puzzles, #4500-3, two in set, ©1965 by the Johnny Gruelle Co., Milton Bradley, $20.00–25.00.

Raggedy Ann picture puzzles, #4855, four pictures, ©1940 by Johnny Gruelle Co., Milton Bradley Co., $90.00–95.00.

Raggedy Ann and Andy railroad picture puzzles, No. 4472, contains 6 puzzles, when all puzzle put together it makes a 9-foot long "train," box is 13" x 18," ©1944 the Johnny Gruelle Co., Milton Bradley Co., $95.00–110.00.

Three Raggedy Ann interlocking puzzles, #4500, ©1954 the Johnny Gruelle Co., by Milton Bradley, $30.00–35.00.

Raggedy Ann Krazy Ikes, "Build 'Em, Bend 'Em, Hang 'Em Anywhere," ©1968 Bobbs-Merrill Co. Inc., by Western Publishing Co., made in Hong Kong, $20.00–25.00.

Raggedy Ann and Andy puzzle, 11" x 16", 60 pieces, ©1989 Macmillan Inc., by Milton Bradley. $12.00–15.00.

Raggedy Ann and Andy mini puzzles, 5" x 7" completed size, 24 pieces, ©1988, 1990 Macmillan Inc., by F.X. Schmid, made in Germany, $5.00–8.00 each.

Raggedy Ann and Andy color TV set, full-color cartoon strips, ©1977 Bobbs-Merrill Co. Inc., by ARCO, $12.00–15.00.

Raggedy Ann and Andy tea set, plastic, ©1976 Bobbs-Merrill Co. Inc., $6.00–8.00 for pieces shown.

Raggedy Ann and Andy finger puppets, 3" vinyl, ©1977 Bobbs-Merrill Co. Inc., by Hallmark Cards, $25.00–30.00 each.

Raggedy Ann and Andy finger puppets, 3" vinyl, ©1972 Bobbs-Merrill Co. Inc., by Knicker-bocker Toy Co Inc., $15.00–20.00 each.

Raggedy Ann and Andy hand puppets, 8½", crocheted yarn, ©1975 Bobbs-Merrill Co. Inc., by R. Dakin & Co., $15.00–20.00 each.

Raggedy Ann and Andy finger puppets, 6" tall, cloth, by Nancy of the Narrows, $20.00–25.00 set.

Raggedy Ann and Andy Learn-To-Dress Doll, both are 14½" x 9", metal with vinyl covers, ©1972 Bobbs-Merrill Co. Inc., by Miner Industries Inc; Ann has close a snap, learn-to-tie a lace, fasten a button; Andy has learn to zip, tie a bow, buckle a belt; $30.00–35.00 each.

Raggedy Andy Stitch 'n' Tie sewing card, 14½" x 11", #7344B, ©1975 Bobbs-Merrill Co. Inc., by Whitman, $12.00–15.00.

Raggedy Ann and Andy tambourine, 6" round, model no. 304, plastic, ©1977 Bobbs-Merrill Co. Inc., by Kingsway, $15.00–18.00.

Raggedy Ann and Andy talking alarm clock, 6½" x 7", plastic, battery operated, made in Hong Kong, $18.00–22.00.

Records and filmstrips, by Gabriel, ©1978 Bobbs-Merrill Co. Inc.; on the left is *Raggedy Ann and Andy and the Kittens*; on the right, *Raggedy Ann and Andy and the Kite;* $10.00–15.00 each.

Raggedy Ann — A Little Folks Game, #4809, ©1954 by the Johnny Gruelle Co., Milton Bradley Company, $30.00–35.00.

Raggedy Ann — A Little Folks Game, #4422, ©1974 Bobbs-Merrill Co. Inc., by Milton Bradley, $18.00–22.00.

Raggedy Ann and Andy Game, #4025, ©1980 Bobbs-Merrill Co. Inc., by Milton Bradley Co., $15.00–18.00.

Raggedy Ann and Andy tea set, nine pieces, metal, CHEIN Playthings No. 432, ©1972 Bobbs-Merrill Co. Inc., $25.00–30.00.

Raggedy Ann and Andy Play Along Xylophone, 9½" long x 6½" wide x 6½" tall, style No. 8079, battery operated, metal and plastic, four changeable records and follow-along songbook, Andy plays xylophone and child uses mallet to play along, ©1978 Azrak-Hamway Inc./Bobbs-Merrill Co. Inc., $35.00–40.00. Xylophone shown out of the box below.

Raggedy Ann talking phone, 9" tall, battery operated, plastic, ©1980 Bobbs-Merrill Co. Inc., $20.00–25.00.

Raggedy Ann musical rocking horse, 6½" tall, an Illco pre-school toy, ©Bobbs-Merrill Co. Inc., by Illfelder Toy Co., $18.00–22.00.

Raggedy Ann See 'N' Say, plastic, by Mattel Preschool, ©1974 Bobbs-Merrill Co. Inc., $30.00–35.00.

Raggedy Ann and Andy squeak toys, 10½", rubber, ©1965 Bobbs-Merrill Co. Inc., manufactured by Arrow Industries Inc., $25.00–30.00 each.

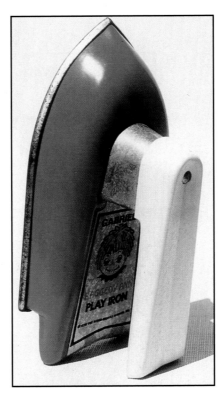

10" Raggedy Ann Vacuum Cleaner Doll, battery operated (batteries go into vacuum), bump-and-go action, ©1973 Bobbs-Merrill Co. Inc., by Nasta Industries, $25.00–30.00.

Raggedy Ann play iron, 6½" long, metal iron with plastic handle, ©1970 Bobbs-Merrill Co. Inc., by Gabriel, $22.00–26.00.

Raggedy Ann night light/ flashlight, 8½" tall, plastic, battery operated, ©1976 Bobbs-Merrill Co. Inc., by Janex Corp., $15.00–18.00.

Raggedy Ann and Andy pinball game, 11" long, plastic, ©1978 Bobbs-Merrill Co. Inc., by Arco, No. 1126, $15.00–18.00.

Raggedy Ann Busy Apron, 12" x 18", ©1969 Bobbs-Merrill Co. Inc., by Whitman, $30.00–35.00.

3" Raggedy Ann wind-up walking doll, plastic, ©1974 Bobbs-Merrill Co. Inc., by Azrak-Hamway Int'l, $15.00–20.00.

Raggedy Ann and Andy kaleidoscope, 9" long, mostly cardboard, ©1974 Bobbs-Merrill Co. Inc., by Hallmark #200PF143-8, $25.00–30.00.

Raggedy Ann and Andy shoeshine kit, ©1974 Bobbs-Merrill Co. Inc., by Janex Corp., $35.00–40.00. Above: Side view of box shows contents of kit.

Raggedy Ann and Andy night light radio, 6½", plastic, by Concept 2000, $30.00–35.00.

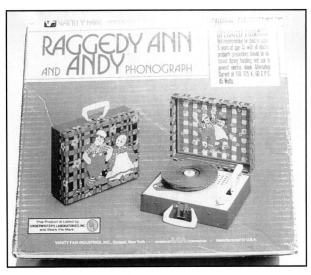

Raggedy Ann and Andy phonograph, model no. 104, ©1974 Bobbs-Merrill Co. Inc., by Vanity Fair, $45.00–55.00.

Raggedy Ann and Andy color 'n' recolor tablecloth, 40" x 36" wipe-off plastic, ©1977 Bobbs-Merrill Co. Inc., by Avalon, $18.00–22.00.

Raggedy Ann sing-a-long radio, 7" x 7", plastic, "It's a radio! It's a sing-a-long! It's a PA system!," ©1975 Bobbs-Merrill Co. Inc., by Concept 2000, $35.00–40.00.

Raggedy Ann's Magic Pebble Game, #4865-A, ©1941 the Johnny Gruelle Co., by Milton Bradley, $35.00–40.00.

Raggedy Ann and Andy Big Sounder, 9½" x 7½", solid-state phonograph, plastic, battery-operated, plays 7" records (33⅓ rpm and 45 rpm), ©1975 Bobbs-Merrill Co. Inc., by Janex #9001, $50.00–55.00.

Raggedy Ann and Andy radio, 6½", plastic, battery operated, ©1973 Bobbs-Merrill Co. Inc., by Philgee International LTD, $15.00–18.00.

Raggedy Ann and Andy Happy Talk phone, 7½", plastic, actually works, phone rests in heart-shaped holder, ©1983 Bobbs-Merrill Co. Inc., by Pan Phone, $35.00–40.00.

Raggedy Ann and Andy tableware, plastic, set for four, box is 10 x 11½", ©1986 Macmillan Inc., by Superior Toy Co., $18.00–20.00.

Raggedy Ann and Andy tea set, steel and plastic, 15" x 18" box, ©1978 Bobbs-Merrill Co. Inc., by Wolverine, $45.00–50.00.

Raggedy Ann and Andy playhouse, plastic, twelve play pieces and play house, ©Knicker-bocker Toy Co. Inc. and Bobbs-Merrill Co. Inc., 1977, $55.00–60.00.

Raggedy Ann sink, 20" x 14½", plastic, ©1978 Bobbs-Merrill Co. Inc., by Hasbro Industries, $45.00–50.00.

Left: **Raggedy Ann play stove,** 11½" x 11", metal; right: **Raggedy Ann play refrigerator,** 15" x 7½", metal; both are ©1970 Bobbs-Merrill Co. Inc., by Gabriel, $40.00–45.00 each.

Songs of Raggedy Ann and Andy, RCA Victor Youth Series, two record set, ©1948 The Johnny Gruelle Co., $30.00–35.00.

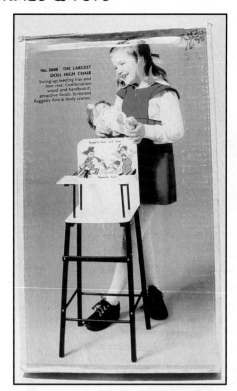

Raggedy Ann, Andy, and Arthur wooden doll high chair, box is 20" x 12", by Roth American Inc., $30.00–35.00.

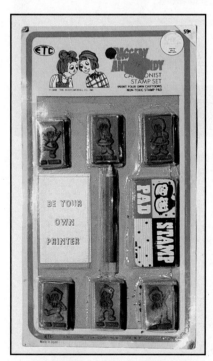

Raggedy Ann and Andy cartoonist stamp set, ©1968 Bobbs-Merrill Co. Inc., by ETC, $18.00–22.00.

Raggedy Ann and Andy camper, 11" x 6", metal and plastic, by Buddy-L Corp., ©Bobbs-Merrill Co. Inc., $35.00–45.00.

Raggedy Ann's play cottage, 13" x 17½", vinyl over cardboard, ©1974 Bobbs-Merrill Co. Inc., by Mattel, $55.00–65.00. Play cottage shown opened in photo below.

Raggedy Ann and Andy three-piece travel set, plastic, includes car, doghouse, camper with 4" Raggedy Ann/Andy dolls and 2" Raggedy Arthur, made in Hong Kong, $35.00–45.00.

HOLIDAY & BIRTHDAY ITEMS

Raggedy Ann and Andy resin ornaments, 3½", ©1990 Macmillan Inc., by Kurt S. Adler Inc., $15.00–20.00 set.

Raggedy Ann and Andy handmade ornaments, 2½" cloth square, $8.00–12.00 set.

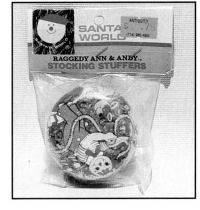

Raggedy Ann and Andy Christmas yoyo, 2" round, ©1980 Bobbs-Merrill Co. Inc., by Kurt S. Adler Inc., $8.00–12.00.

18" Raggedy Ann and Andy Christmas stocking, made of cloth, ©1976 Brite Star MFG Co., $2.00–3.00.

4" Raggedy Ann and 4½" Raggedy Andy wooden ornaments, both have yarn hair, Ann ©1980; Andy ©1983 Bobbs-Merrill Co. Inc., by Kurt S. Adler Inc.; $15.00–18.00 each.

Left: **Raggedy Ann and Andy ornament,** wooden dolls with yarn hair on metal bike, ©1980 Bobbs-Merrill Co. Inc., by Kurt S. Adler Inc., $15.00–20.00. Right: **Raggedy Andy wooden ornaments,** 4" and 4½", yarn hair, ©1980 Bobbs-Merrill Co. Inc., by Kurt S. Adler Inc., $15.00–18.00 each.

Left: **Raggedy Ann wooden ornaments,** yarn hair. Left: 3½", ©1980 Bobbs-Merrill Co. Inc; right: 4½", ©1983 Bobbs-Merrill Co. Inc. Both by Kurt S. Adler Inc.; $15.00–18.00 each.

Right: **3½" Raggedy Arthur wooden ornament,** yarn hair, ©1980 Bobbs-Merrill Co. Inc., by Kurt S. Adler Inc., $25.00–30.00.

4" Alexander Graham Wolf ornament, wooden with yarn hair, ©1980 Bobbs-Merrill Co. Inc., by Kurt S. Adler Inc., $25.00–30.00.

4½" Raggedy Ann and Andy wooden ornaments, ©1992 Macmillan Inc., $15.00–20.00 for set.

Raggedy Ann and Andy wooden ornaments, 5" Andy, 4" Ann, ©1990 Macmillan Inc., by Kurt S. Adler Inc., $15.00–20.00 for set.

6" Raggedy Ann and Andy wooden ornaments, ©1992 Macmillan Inc., by Kurt S. Adler Inc., $15.00–20.00 for set.

Raggedy Ann wooden ornaments, 6½" and 6", yarn hair, both are ©1993, $8.00–10.00 each.

Raggedy Ann and Andy Christmas 1975 glass ball ornaments, approx. 2" diameter, by Hallmark, $35.00–40.00 for set.

6" Raggedy Ann and Andy wooden ornaments, ©1992 Macmillan Inc., $12.00–15 for set.

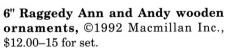

3½" Raggedy Ann and Andy figurine ornaments, ©1975 Bobbs-Merrill Co. Inc., by Hallmark Tree Trimmer Collection (Ann #250QX159-1, Andy #250QX160-1), $150.00–200.00 each.

Raggedy Ann and Andy Christmas cards, 25 cards, by Hallmark, #200PX405, $18.00–22.00.

Raggedy Andy Halloween costume, cotton and rayon outfit, plastic mask, one-piece blue outfit, Ben Cooper, ©1965 Bobbs-Merrill Co. Inc., $22.00–26.00.

Raggedy Ann Halloween costume, cotton and rayon, plastic mask, one-piece red outfit, Ben Cooper, ©1965 Bobbs-Merrill Co. Inc., $22.00−26.00.

Raggedy Ann Halloween costume, rayon, one-piece dress, plastic mask, Ben Cooper, ©1965 Bobbs-Merrill Co. Inc., $22.00–26.00.

Raggedy Ann Halloween costume, one-piece vinyl dress, plastic mask, Ben Cooper, ©1982 Bobbs-Merrill Co. Inc., $12.00–16.00.

Raggedy Ann Halloween costume, two-piece red vinyl vest and skirt outfit, plastic mask, Ben Cooper ©1973 Bobbs-Merrill Co. Inc., $18.00–22.00.

Raggedy Ann Halloween costume, two-piece outfit, red rayon skit, white vinyl vest, plastic mask with pink hair, Ben Cooper, ©1973 Bobbs-Merrill Co. Inc., $22.00–25.00.

Raggedy Ann and Andy cloth mask, 15" long, Collegeville Costumes, ©1991 Macmillan Inc., $20.00–25.00 each.

Raggedy Ann costume, vinyl costume, plastic mask, Collegeville, ©1991 Macmillan Inc., $10.00–12.00.

Raggedy Ann Santa bell, 4" tall, ceramic, "Napcoware import Japan," $10.00–12.00.

Raggedy Ann and Andy yarn and trim, 8" cardboard gift card with yarn, ©1974 Bobbs-Merrill Co. Inc., by Hallmark 49XTM202-3, $12.00–15.00.

Raggedy Ann and Andy styrofoam ornaments, 3½" to 4", cloth clothes, yarn hair, $2.00–4.00 each.

Left: **5" Raggedy Andy wooden ornament,** pull string to make legs and arms move, ©1981 Bobbs-Merrill Co. Inc., by Kurt S. Adler, $15.00–18.00. Right: **5" Raggedy Andy wooden ornament,** ©1984 Bobbs-Merrill Co. Inc., by Kurt S. Adler, $10.00–12.00.

Raggedy Ann and Andy styrofoam ornaments, approx. 3½", cloth clothes, yarn hair, $2.00–4.00 each.

2¾" Raggedy Ann and Andy ceramic ornaments, hand painted, notice facial variations in sets, ©1980 Bobbs-Merrill Co. Inc., by Schmid, $25.00–30.00 set.

22" Christmas decorations, cardboard, ©1978, 1982 Bobbs-Merrill Co. Inc., $8.00–10.00 each.

Christmas decoration, cardboard, ©1978, 1982 Bobbs-Merrill Co. Inc., ice skating Raggedy Ann is 21" long, $8.00–10.00.

155

Raggedy Ann and Andy Christmas stockings, 12" tall, material with vinyl appliqués, ©The Bobbs-Merrill Co. Inc., $15.00–20.00 each.

Raggedy Andy glass ball ornaments, 3" diameter, ©1973 Bobbs-Merrill Co. Inc., by Corning Glass Works, $12.00–15.00 each.

Left: **Raggedy Ann Valentines,** four each of three different designs, ©1974, 1976 Bobbs-Merrill Co. Inc., by Hallmark, #150BV3-3, $20.00–25.00. Right: **Raggedy Ann and Andy Valentines,** box of 30, ©1986 Macmillan Inc., by Hallmark, $12.00–15.00.

Raggedy Ann and Andy's Secret Trip — A Birthday Story card, 9" tall, stick-on pictures, ©1974 Bobbs-Merrill Co. Inc., by Hallmark #75B150-4, $12.00–15.00.

Raggedy Ann and Andy pop-out/stand-up card, 9" tall, ©1974 Bobbs-Merrill Co. Inc., by Hallmark #100F706-1, $12.00–15.00.

Raggedy Ann's Easter Parade Egg Decorating Kit, Hinkle Easter Products, ©1992 #16921, 1992 Macmillan Inc., $8.00–12.00.

Raggedy Ann and Andy pop-out/stand-up card, 9" tall, ©1974 Bobbs-Merrill Co. Inc., by Hallmark #100F707-1, $12.00–15.00.

Raggedy Ann and Andy Mobile Just for You card, 9" tall, Raggedy characters punch out to make a mobile, ©1974 Bobbs-Merrill Co. Inc., by Hallmark #150F702-1, $15.00–18.00.

Raggedy Ann and Andy game card, 9" tall, ©1974 Bobbs-Merrill Co. Inc., by Hallmark 150F703-1, punch out pieces to play game, includes spinner, $15.00–18.00.

Raggedy Ann and Andy Go to the Carnival card, 9", "A delightful story with stick-on pictures and a stick-on puzzle!," ©1974 Bobbs-Merrill Co. Inc., by Hallmark #150F704-1, $15.00–18.00.

Your Growing-Up Chart, 9", ©1974 Bobbs-Merrill Co. Inc., by Hallmark, $15.00–18.00.

Left: **Happy Birthday 1 year old card,** 6½", ©Bobbs-Merrill Company Inc., by Hallmark, $10.00–12.00. Right: **For a Little Girl Who's 1 card,** 7½", ©1974 Bobbs-Merrill Company Inc., by Hallmark, $10.00–12.00.

A Money card from Sugarplum Land!, 9", ©1974 Bobbs-Merrill Co. Inc., by Hallmark, $18.00–20.00.

Left: **For a Boy Who's 1 card,** 6½", ©1976 Bobbs-Merrill Co. Inc., by Hallmark, $10.00–12.00. Right: **Raggedy Ann and Andy Country Picnic Coloring Book,** 6" x 5", ©1973 Bobbs-Merrill Co. Inc., by Hallmark, $8.00–10.00.

Left: **Daughter You're Very Special! card,** 6", ©Bobbs-Merrill Company Inc., by Hallmark, $10.00–12.00. Right: **For A Sweet Daughter,** 6½", ©1974 Bobbs-Merrill Co. Inc., by Ambassador, $10.00–12.00.

Left: **For a Little 2 Year Old With Love,** 6½", ©Bobbs-Merrill Co. Inc., by Hallmark, $10.00–12.00. Right: **Now You're 2,** 7", ©1975 Bobbs-Merrill Co. Inc., by Hallmark, $10.00–12.00.

Left: **For a Sweet 3 Year Old,** 6½", ©Bobbs-Merrill Co. Inc., by Hallmark, $10.00–12.00. Right: **For A Sweet 3 Year Old,** 7½", ©1974 Bobbs-Merrill Co. Inc., by Hallmark, $10.00–12.00.

Left: **For You Because You're 4,** 6½", ©Bobbs-Merrill Co. Inc., by Hallmark, $10.00–12.00. Right: **For You Because You're 4,** 7½", ©1974 Bobbs-Merrill Co. Inc., by Hallmark, $10.00–12.00.

Left: **For A Little Miss Who's 5,** 6½", ©Bobbs-Merrill Co. Inc., by Hallmark, $10.00–12.00. Right: **Now You're 5,** 7½", ©1974 Bobbs-Merrill Co. Inc., by Hallmark, $10.00–12.00.

Left: **You're 6 Today!** 7½", ©1974 Bobbs-Merrill Co. Inc., by Hallmark, $10.00–12.00. Right: **To a Sweet Niece card,** 7½", ©1974 Bobbs-Merrill Co. Inc., by Hallmark, $10.00–12.00.

Left: **For A Grandson's 1st Valentine's Day card,** 7", ©1990 Macmillan Inc., by Hallmark, $8.00–10.00. Center: **For a Special Granddaughter, a Birthday wish form Raggedy Ann card,** 7½", ©1988 Macmillan Inc., by Hallmark, $8.00–10.00. Right: **For My Daughter valentine card,** 7½", ©1990 Macmillan Inc., by Hallmark, $8.00–10.00.

Left: **For a Sweet Great-Granddaughter Here's Raggedy Ann card,** 8", ©Bobbs-Merrill Company Inc., by Hallmark, $10.00–12.00. Right: **For Your Birthday Grandson, Here's Raggedy Andy card,** 8", ©Bobbs-Merrill Company Inc., by Hallmark, $10.00–12.00.

Left: **Happy Birthday to a Very Special Niece card,** 7½", ©1990 Macmillan Inc., Ambassador, $10.00–12.00. Right: **For a Special Granddaughter card,** 8½", ©1991 Macmillan Inc., by Ambassador, $10.00–12.00.

Left: **On your Birthday, Here's Raggedy Ann card,** 9", ©Bobbs-Merrill Company Inc., by Hallmark, $10.00–12.00. Right: **Hi! I'm Raggedy Ann and Look What I've Got... card,** 7½", ©Bobbs-Merrill Company Inc., by Hallmark, $10.00–12.00.

Left: **Beloved Belindy and the Chocolate Chip Day,** 10" storybook card, ©1974 Bobbs-Merrill Co. Inc., by Hallmark, $30.00–35.00. Center: **Uncle Clem's Carnival,** 10" storybook card, ©1974 Bobbs-Merrill Co. Inc., by Hallmark, $25.00–30.00. Right: **Henny's Picnic,** 10" storybook card, ©1974 Bobbs-Merrill Co. Inc., by Hallmark, $25.00–30.00.

Left: **Marcella Meets Raggedy Ann;** center: **How Raggedy Ann Got Her Candy Heart;** right: **Raggedy Andy's Doll Hospital;** all are 10" storybook cards, ©1974 Bobbs-Merrill Co. Inc., by Hallmark, $25.00–30.00 each.

Left: **For Granddaughter Christmas card,** 7", ©1974 Bobbs-Merrill Co. Inc., by Hallmark, $12.00–15.00. Right: **A Wish For A Niece Who's A Real Little Doll... Christmas card,** 5½", ©Bobbs-Merrill Company Inc., by Hallmark, $12.00–15.00.

Left: **Just for You, Valentine card,** 5½", ©1976 Bobbs-Merrill Co. Inc., by Hallmark, $10.00–12.00. Right: **Raggedy Ann and Andy Valentine card,** 6½", ©1975 Bobbs-Merrill Co. Inc., by Hallmark, $10.00–12.00.

Raggedy Ann and Andy A Valentine For You With Finger Puppets You Can Play With! card, 8" tall, ©Forget-Me-Not Cards, #25V1001-4H, $10.00–12.00.

Left: **A Valentine For You card;** center: **A Valentine Hi;** right: **Raggedy Ann Valentine;** all are 5½" tall, ©1975 Bobbs-Merrill Co. Inc., by Hallmark, $10.00–12.00 each.

Left: **Congratulations... baby card,** 6½", ©1976 Bobbs-Merrill Co. Inc., by Hallmark, $12.00–15.00. Right: **A Valentine for a Dear Niece,** 7", ©Greetings Inc., $3.00–6.00.

Raggedy Ann and Andy gift card, 3¼" square, ©Bobbs-Merrill Co. Inc., by Hallmark #16GE152-1, $5.00–8.00.

Left: **Raggedy Ann mini puzzle party favor,** 6" x 4", #35PF1623; right: **Raggedy Ann and Andy party favor puzzle,** 6½" x 5", #50PF1506; both are ©Bobbs-Merrill Company Inc., by Hallmark, $12.00–16.00 each.

Raggedy Ann party favor puzzle, 6½" tall, includes envelope to hold pieces, ©1974 Bobbs-Merrill Co. Inc., by Hallmark, $15.00–18.00.

Top row: Left: **Happy Birthday Raggedy Ann and Andy gift card,** 3¼" square, ©1974 Bobbs-Merrill Co. Inc., by Hallmark, $5.00–8.00. Center: **For You Raggedy Ann gift card,** 3½" x 2¾", ©Bobbs-Merrill Co. Inc., by Hallmark, $5.00–8.00. Right: **For You Raggedy Andy gift card,** 3½" x 2¾", ©Bobbs-Merrill Co. Inc., by Hallmark, $5.00–8.00.

Bottom row: Left: **Raggedy Ann and Andy gift card,** ©1974 Bobbs-Merrill Co. Inc., by Hallmark, $5.00–8.00. Right: **For You Raggedy Ann and Andy gift card,** 3½", © Bobbs-Merrill Co. Inc., by Hallmark, $5.00–8.00.

Left: **Raggedy Ann wrapping paper,** by Hallmark; right: **Raggedy Ann and Andy gift wrap,** by Tuttle Press; $15.00–18.00 each.

Raggedy Ann and Andy Christmas wrap, paper on left made by Hallmark, $12.00–15.00 each.

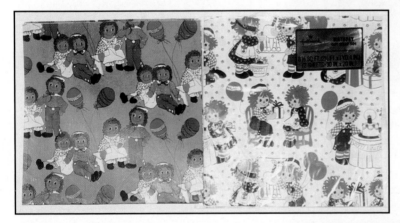

Raggedy Ann and Andy birthday wrap, paper on right by Hallmark, $12.00–15.00 each.

Left: **Raggedy Andy wrap,** by Hallmark; right: **Raggedy Ann and Andy wrap,** by Ambassador; $12.00–15.00 each.

Left: **Raggedy Ann wrap,** by Hallmark; right: **Raggedy Ann and Andy wrap,** by Hallmark; $12.00–15.00 each.

Raggedy Ann and Andy Christmas wrap, by Hallmark, $12.00–15.00.

Left: **Raggedy Ann nut cups,** pack of 8, ©Bobbs-Merrill Company Inc., by Hallmark, #100NC162-3, $15.00–18.00. Right: **Raggedy Ann and Andy nut cups,** pack of 8, ©Bobbs-Merrill Company Inc., by Hallmark, #75NC140-5, $15.00–18.00.

Raggedy Ann and Andy centerpieces. Left: ©Bobbs-Merrill Company Inc., by Hallmark, #175CP140-5; right: 11½", ©1974 Bobbs-Merrill Co. Inc., by Hallmark, #200CP143-8; $18.00–24.00 each.

Raggedy Ann and Andy centerpieces. Left: ©Bobbs-Merrill Company Inc., by Hallmark, #175CP140-5; right: 11½", ©1974 Bobbs-Merrill Co. Inc., by Hallmark, #200CP143-8; $18.00–24.00 each.

Left: **Raggedy Ann and Andy Freewheeling Fun centerpiece**, 11½" tall, ©1978 Bobbs-Merrill Co. Inc., by Hallmark, #225CP243-1, $20.00–25.00. Right: **Raggedy Ann and Andy Birthday centerpiece**, ©1988 Paper Art Co., Inc., #26-520, $10.00–14.00.

Left: **Raggedy Ann and Andy paper cups**, 3" tall, eight cups, ©Bobbs-Merrill Company Inc., by Hallmark, $12.00–15.00. Right: **Raggedy "look-a-like" paper cups**, Ambassador, $3.00–5.00.

Raggedy Ann paper placemats, eight per pack, © Bobbs-Merrill Co. Inc., by Hallmark, #100MT1623, $15.00–18.00.

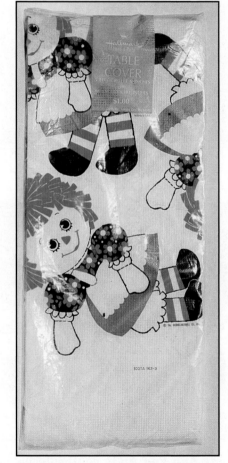

Raggedy Ann paper napkins, 6½" square, 20 per pack, by Hallmark, $10.00–12.00.

Raggedy Ann and Andy paper tablecloth, 60" x 102", ©Bobbs-Merrill Company Inc., by Hallmark, $14.00–18.00.

Raggedy Ann plastic plates, 9" round, four in package, by Hallmark, #100DP24-2, circa 1973, $15.00`–18.00.

Raggedy Ann paper plates, 9" round, eight in pack, by Ambassador Cards, $10.00–12.00.

Raggedy Ann and Andy paper napkins, 6½" square, 20 per pack, by Hallmark, $10.00–12.00 each.

Raggedy Ann and Andy birthday party set, includes large and small plates, cups, napkins, hats, and invitations, all are ©1988 Macmillan Inc., by Paper Art, $25.00–30.00 for set.

Left: **Raggedy Ann and Andy paper tablecloth,** 54" x 90", by Reed's, circa 1940s–1950s, $45.00–50.00. Right: **Raggedy Ann party invitation,** 5" tall, ©Bobbs-Merrill Co. Inc., by Hallmark, #60PM162-3, $2.00–3.00.

Raggedy Ann first day of issue cover, Christmas 1978, Colorado "silk" cachet, $15.00–20.00.

Left: **Raggedy Ann notecard,** 5", ©Bobbs-Merrill Co. Inc., by Hallmark, $5.00–8.00. Top right: **Raggedy Ann self-adhesive seals,** for baby shower, 2½" square, ten in pack, ©Hallmark, $5.00–8.00. Bottom right: **Raggedy Ann and Andy gift card,** 1¾" square, hand-made, Original Treasure Masters of Boston, $3.00–5.00.

Two Raggedy Ann and Andy gift boxes, cardboard, ©1974 Bobbs-Merrill Co. Inc., by Hallmark, #175EGB1543, $18.00–22.00.

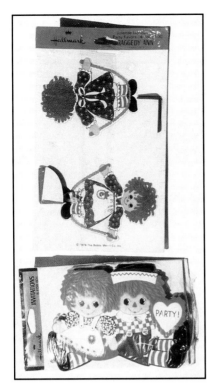

Top: **Raggedy Ann honeycomb party favors,** four in pack, ©1974 Bobbs-Merrill Co. Inc., by Hallmark #100PF146-9, $18.00–22.00. Bottom: **Raggedy Ann and Andy party invitations,** pack of eight, ©Bobbs-Merrill Company Inc., by Hallmark #60PM140-5, $10.00–15.00.

Raggedy Ann and Andy gift bags, two bags plus self-adhesive seals, 16" x 11½", ©1974 Bobbs-Merrill Co. Inc., by Hallmark, $25.00–30.00.

Raggedy Ann Christmas light decoration, 15" tall, plastic, light fits into back, ©1973 Bobbs-Merrill Co. Inc., $25.00–30.00.

Raggedy Ann and Andy glass ball ornaments, approx. 1½" diameter, ©1974 Bobbs-Merrill Co. Inc., by Hallmark, $15.00–20.00 each.

Raggedy Ann Santa candle, 7" tall, "Christmas Novelty candle, W.T. Grant Co. NY" on paper sticker, $15.00–20.00.

Raggedy Ann and Andy Christmas figurines, 5" tall, ceramic, ©1974 Bobbs-Merrill Co. Inc., $10.00–12.00 set.

Left: **12½" Raggedy Ann and Andy sewing card,** ©1974 Bobbs-Merrill Co. Inc., by Hallmark, #100PF143-8, $20.00–25.00. Right: **13" Raggedy Ann gift box,** cardboard, by Hallmark, $12.00–15.00.

Raggedy Ann decal on sand dollar, 3" diameter. $12.00–15.00.

Raggedy Andy glass ball ornaments, 2½" diameter, set of six, ©1973 Bobbs-Merrill Co. Inc., by Corning Glass, $20.00–25.00 set.

Raggedy Andy glass ball ornaments, 2½" diameter, set of six, ©1974 Bobbs-Merrill Co. Inc., by Corning Glass, $20.00–25.00 set.

Raggedy Ann and Andy animated Christmas dolls, 30" tall, cloth dolls with yarn hair, their candle lights up and arms and heads rotate when plugged in, probably made for store display, very hard to find, $250.00–275.00 each. Close-up of animated dolls shown below.

LAMPS

Raggedy Andy lamp, 10" tall, vinyl and plastic, ©Bobbs-Merrill Co. Inc., Famous Juvenile Products by Lydia Div. of Universal Lamp Co. Japan, $20.00–25.00.

Raggedy Ann and Andy desk lamp, 6½" to top of figurines, plastic and vinyl, moveable extension arm, ©1977 Bobbs-Merrill Co. Inc., by Vanity Fair Ind. Inc., $25.00–30.00.

Raggedy Ann ceramic night light, 4½" tall, by I.W. Rice & Co., $8.00–12.00.

Raggedy Ann and Andy night light, 4", vinyl, $8.00–12.00.

Raggedy Ann and Andy nursery lamp with night light, ©1974 Bobbs-Merrill Co. Inc., by Dolly Toy, $30.00–35.00.

Raggedy Ann and Andy lamp, 12" lamp with night light, plastic, ©1980 Bobbs-Merrill Co. Inc., by Dolly Toy, $25.00–30.00.

Raggedy Ann and Andy lamp, 11" to top of figurines, ceramic, $15.00–20.00.

Raggedy Ann and Andy musical lamp, 11", wooden, when music plays Ann and Andy go up and down on seesaw, ©1973 Bobbs-Merrill Co. Inc., $20.00–25.00.

Raggedy Ann and Andy lamps, cloth doll on plastic block, plastic base, ©1973 Bobbs-Merrill Co. Inc., $10.00–15.00 each.

Raggedy Ann and Andy ceramic lamps, 15" tall to top of ceramic figurine, very large and heavy lamps, $30.00–45.00 each.

Raggedy Ann head lamp, 11½", plastic with yarn hair, $35.00–40.00.

MISCELLANEOUS ITEMS

Raggedy Ann and Andy figurine, 3" tall, sitting on log, paper sticker "Norleans Korea," $8.00–12.00.

Raggedy Ann and Andy figurines, 4" tall, ©1974 the Bobbs-Merrill Co. Inc., $10.00–15.00 pair.

Raggedy Ann and Andy metal serving tray, 13½" square, by Pritchard, designed by Daher, made in England, $18.00–22.00.

Raggedy Ann and Andy's Fun-filled Playtime Box, Whitman, ©1976 the Bobbs-Merrill Co. Inc., contains three storybooks, paperdolls, frame tray puzzle, coloring book, 16 crayons, and magic slate pad, $25.00–30.00.

Raggedy Ann and Andy wall hangings, 28½" tall, pressboard, $35.00–40.00 each.

Raggedy Ann and Andy mobiles, 13½" tall, ©1972 Japan, Fitz & Floyd Inc., $25.00–30.00 each.

Raggedy Ann and Andy wall decoration,
17" x 14½", cardboard, $8.00–12.00.

**Raggedy Ann and Andy cardboard playhouse cottage
and wood furniture,** cottage and furniture you assemble,
©1980 the Bobbs-Merrill Co. Inc., $30.00–35.00. Below are
assembly instructions for playhouse and wooden furniture.

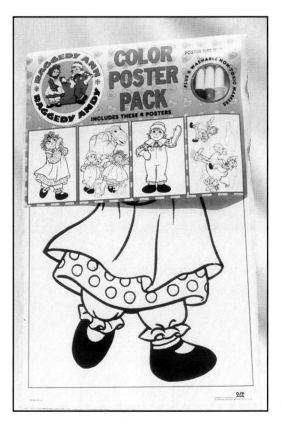

**Raggedy Ann and Andy Color Poster
Pack,** 11" x 17", includes four posters and four
pens, ©1993 Macmillan Inc., O.S.P. Publishing
Inc., $10.00–12.00.

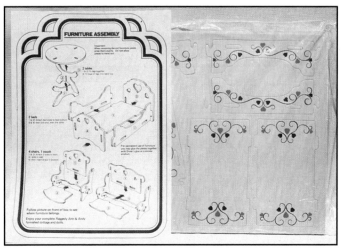

Raggedy Ann and Andy clock, 5" round, plastic case with glass face and wooden feet, battery operated, ©1992 Macmillan Inc., made in Japan by K. Company, $50.00–60.00.

Above: **Raggedy Ann corkboard,** 22" tall, no markings, $25.00–30.00. Below: **Raggedy Andy corkboard,** 23" tall, © The Bobbs-Merrill Co. Inc., by Manton Cork Corp., $25.00–30.00.

Raggedy Ann and Andy glasses, 6" tall, Ann on one side, Andy on other, $18.00–22.00 each.

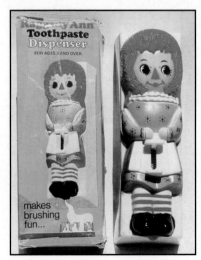

Raggedy Ann toothpaste dispenser, 8" tall, plastic, ©1973 the Bobbs-Merrill Co. Inc., by Enco Industries, Hong Kong, $15.00–20.00.

Left: **McCall's pattern #4268 for 36" Raggedy Ann and Andy dolls and child's apron,** ©1974 the Bobbs-Merrill Co. Inc., $10.00–12.00. Right: **McCall's pattern #628 for 36" Raggedy Ann and Andy dolls and child's apron,** ©1982 the Bobbs-Merrill Co. Inc. $8.00–10.00.

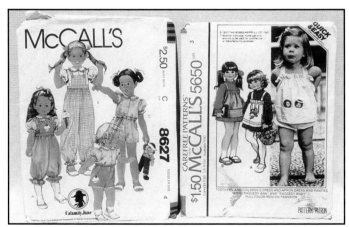

Left: **McCall's pattern #8627,** shows Andy doll on pattern sleeve but doll pattern not included, ©1983. $2.00–4.00. Right: **McCall's pattern #5650,** pattern for child's dress, apron, panties with full color Raggedy Ann and Andy transfers, ©1977 the Bobbs-Merrill Co. Inc., $12.00–14.00.

Left: **McCall's pattern #5713,** 10/15/20/25" Raggedy Ann and Andy dolls, ©1977 the Bobbs-Merrill Co. Inc., $8.00–10.00. Right: **McCall's pattern #2531,** 15/20/25" Raggedy Ann and Andy dolls, ©1970 the Bobbs-Merrill Co. Inc., $10.00–12.00.

Left: **McCall's pattern #623,** 10/15/20/25" Raggedy Ann and Andy dolls, ©1982 the Bobbs-Merrill Co. Inc., $8.00–10.00. Right: **McCall's pattern #6941,** 15/20/25" Raggedy Ann and Andy dolls, ©1963 the Bobbs-Merrill Co. Inc., $15.00–18.00.

Left: **McCall's pattern #3001,** toddler's dress, pinafore, and panties with transfer for Raggedy Ann pocket, ©1971 the Bobbs-Merrill Co. Inc., $10.00–12.00. Right: **McCall's pattern #2529,** child's jacket, top, pants, bloomers, and pinafore with transfer to make Raggedy Ann badge, ©1970 the Bobbs-Merrill Co. Inc., $10.00–12.00.

Left: **McCall's pattern #5418,** Little Raggedy dolls, 12" or 16", ©1991 Macmillan Inc., $10.00–15.00. Right: **McCall's pattern #2530,** child's dress and jumper with transfer for Raggedy Ann pocket, ©1970 the Bobbs-Merrill Co. Inc., $10.00–12.00.

Left: **McCall's pattern #5616,** misses t-shirt with Raggedy Ann and Andy color transfer, ©1977 the Bobbs-Merrill Co. Inc., $8.00–10.00. Right: **McCall's pattern #2240,** child's nightgown and pajamas with color Raggedy Ann and Andy transfer, ©1985 Macmillan Inc., $6.00–8.00.

Left: **McCall's pattern #7223,** girl's and boy's costumes, ©1964 the Bobbs-Merrill Co. Inc., $20.00–25.00. Right: **McCall's pattern #5254,** adult/child's costumes, ©1976 the Bobbs-Merrill Co. Inc., $15.00–18.00.

McCall's pattern #820, for 19" Raggedy Ann and Andy dolls, 1940, same pattern, shows two different versions, $35.00–40.00 each.

Raggedy Ann and Andy pop-up sponges, 4¾" tall, expands in water, ©1987 Macmillan Inc. $8.00–10.00.

Left: **Raggedy Ann Soft Sponge Bath Mitt,** 7" tall, ©1980 Bobbs-Merrill Co. Inc., by Brooklyn Products; right: **Raggedy Andy Soft Sponge Bath Mitt,** 7" tall, ©1978 Bobbs-Merrill Co. Inc., by Fine Industries; $10.00–15.00 each.

Raggedy Ann's Spray Starch, 9" tall metal can, net wt 22oz., by the Faultless Starch Co., ©1967 Bobbs-Merrill Co. Inc., made in USA, $25.00–35.00.

Raggedy Ann and Andy candy cake decorations, 20 pieces, by Snow Crest Foods, ©1978 Bobbs-Merrill Co. Inc., $8.00–12.00.

Raggedy Ann paperweight, 3½" tall, should be holding something in outstretched hand, felt bottom, sand-filled, ©1972 Fitz & Floyd Inc., $10.00–15.00.

Raggedy Ann and Andy cookie cutters, 4½" tall, Hallmark 75PF140-9, $20.00–25.00.

Raggedy Ann and Andy snapshot album, 8" x 10½", press board with material cover, ©1945 The Johnny Gruelle Co., $35.00–40.00.

Raggedy Ann and Andy View Master Classic Tales, 21 stereo pictures, ©1971 Bobbs-Merrill Co. Inc., GAF Corporation, $18.00–22.00.

Raggedy Ann orange and grapefruit sections, R. Ann Corporation distributors, 1602, $8.00–10.00.

Raggedy Ann and Andy Superflex dolls, 6" tall, by Lakeside, No. 8146, ©1967 the Bobbs-Merrill Co. Inc., $30.00–35.00.

Watering can, 9" tall, metal, ©1973 Bobbs-Merrill Co. Inc., by CHEIN Playthings, $30.00–35.00.

Storybooks and records, 45 rpm records and read-along story, Hallmark, $30.00–35.00 each. Above left: **Raggedy Ann and Andy on a Trip to the Stars,** 300QN-117-1. Above right: **Raggedy Ann and Andy Visit the Kingdom of "Every Wish,"** 300QN-120-1. Below left: **Raggedy Ann and Andy go to Cookietown,** 300QN-122-1.

Storybooks and records, 45 rpm records and read-along story, Hallmark, $30.00–35.00 each. Above left: **Raggedy Ann and Andy on a Journey Beneath the Enchanted Pond,** 300QN-119-1. Above right: **Raggedy Ann and Andy in Dreamland,** 300QN-121-1. Below left: **Raggedy Ann and Andy meet Dizzy Izzy and the Witch,** 300QN-118-1,

Raggedy Ann and Andy Fabriche Figurines, 8½" tall, by Kurt S. Adler Inc., 1995, $80.00–90.00 pair.

Raggedy Ann and Andy figurine, 6¼" tall, ceramic, felt bottom stamped "©1972 the Bobbs-Merrill Co. Inc., World Rights Reserved, Determined Productions Inc," paper sticker "Hand made in Japan," $18.00–22.00.

Raggedy Ann and Andy drinking cup, 3¾" tall, hard plastic, both sides shown, © Bobbs-Merrill Co. Inc., $15.00–20.00.

Raggedy Ann and Andy juice glass, 4" tall, ©1972 Bobbs-Merrill Co. Inc., $10.00–12.00 each.

Raggedy Ann and Andy cups, 3¼" tall, ceramic, made in Japan, $10.00–12.00 each.

Raggedy Ann wind chime, 6" tall, ceramic bisque, legs hangs down inside to clank when the wind blows, by Knobler, Japan (paper sticker), $28.00–32.00.

Raggedy Ann foam bendee doll, 13½" tall, probably made for store display, ©1968 Bobbs-Merrill Co. Inc., manufacturing by Lakeside Ind Inc., licenced by Newfeld LTD of England, $60.00–65.00.

Raggedy Ann and Andy magnetic stickers, sizes from 2½" to 8" tall, five per pack, ©1978 Bobbs-Merrill Co. Inc., $12.00–15.00 each.

Raggedy Ann and Andy magnetic stickers, sizes from 2½" to 8" tall, five per pack, ©1978 Bobbs-Merrill Co. Inc., $12.00–15.00 each.

Raggedy Ann and Andy Christmas Party album, ©1976, 1978, 1980 Bobbs-Merrill Co. Inc., by Kid Stuff, $8.00–10.00.

Raggedy Ann and Andy Pop Concert album, ©1976, 1978, 1980 Bobbs-Merrill Co. Inc., by Kid Stuff, $8.00–10.00.

Raggedy Ann and Andy Bend & Stretch album, ©1976, 1978, 1980 Bobbs-Merrill Co. Inc., by Kid Stuff, $8.00–10.00.

Raggedy Ann and Andy Birthday Party album, ©1976, 1978, 1980 Bobbs-Merrill Co. Inc., by Kid Stuff, $8.00–10.00.

Raggedy Ann and Andy Dance Party album, ©1976, 1978, 1980 Bobbs-Merrill Co. Inc., by Kid Stuff, $8.00–10.00.

Raggedy Ann and Andy Alphabet & Numbers album, ©1976, 1978, 1980 Bobbs-Merrill Co. Inc., by Kid Stuff, $8.00–10.00.

Raggedy Ann and Andy Telling Time is Fun album, ©1976, 1978, 1980 Bobbs-Merrill Co. Inc., by Kid Stuff, $8.00–10.00.

Raggedy Ann and Andy Happiness Album, Limited Edition Collector series, phono picture disk, ©1976, 1978, 1980 Bobbs-Merrill Co. Inc., by Kid Stuff, $25.00–30.00.

Raggedy Ann and Andy printer's blocks, sizes from 1" to 1½", $15.00–20.00 each.

6" Raggedy Ann and Andy cookie dough figures, marked "VINT 1978," $12.00–15.00 pair.

Raggedy Ann and Andy cookie dough figures, Ann is 3½", Andy is 4", marked "Handcrafted by The Dough Girls 1977," $20.00–25.00 set.

Raggedy Ann and Andy cookie dough figures, all are marked "VINT 1978," 2" pair, $10.00–12.00; 1" pair, $10.00–12.00; ¾" pair, $8.00–10.00.

Raggedy Ann and Andy cookie cutters, 4" tall, plastic, Ervan Guttman Co., $15.00–18.00 pair.

Left: **Raggedy Ann needlepoint,** 11" square; right: **Raggedy Andy needlepoint,** 11" square, by Needle Nuts Jr.; $8.00–12.00 each.

Raggedy Ann and Andy needlepoint, 15" square design area, ©1972 Bobbs-Merrill Co. Inc., marked "tina 401," $20.00–25.00.

Raggedy Ann and Andy needlepoint, 16" x 20", Tina of California #5025, $25.00–30.00.

Raggedy Ann and Andy needlepoint, 16" x 15", ©1972 Bobbs-Merrill Co. Inc., #405, $20.00–25.00.

Left: **Raggedy Andy hook rug canvas,** 20" x 27", by Spinnerin Yarn Co., $20.00–25.00.
Right: **Raggedy Ann and Andy hook rug canvas,** 30" x 40", by Spinnerin Yarn Co., $35.00–40.00.

Raggedy Ann hook rug, 20" x 27" by Spinnerin Yarn Co., $20.00–25.00.

Raggedy Ann and Andy latch hook pillow canvas, 15" square, ©1977 Bobbs-Merrill Co. Inc., by Contessa, $18.00–22.00 each.

Raggedy Ann and Andy Krewel Kidds, 16" square wall hanging or pillow, by Sew 'n' Tell, $15.00–18.00 each.

Raggedy Ann and Andy ceramic figurines, 3" tall, ©1981 Bobbs-Merrill Co. Inc., $20.00–25.00 set.

Raggedy Ann and Andy ceramic figurines, 3½" tall, ©1978 Bobbs-Merrill Co. Inc., by Pussy Willow Creations, $10.00–15.00 each.

Raggedy Ann and Andy ceramic figurines, 7" tall, ©1975 Bobbs-Merrill Co. Inc., $15.00–20.00 set.

Read-along book and 45 rpm record, ©1980 Bobbs-Merrill Co. Inc., by Kid Stuff, $12.00–15.00 each. Top row, left to right: **Raggedy Ann's Birthday Party** and **Raggedy Ann and Andy Book of Manners;** bottom row, left to right: **Raggedy Ann and Andy's Alphabet, Raggedy Ann and Andy at the Circus,** and **Raggedy Ann and Andy's Rainy Day Songs & Games.**

Raggedy Ann and Andy Book of Manners, read-along book with cassette tape, Kid Stuff records, $15.00–18.00.

Left: **Raggedy Ann and Andy cookie cutters,** 8" plastic, ©Bobbs-Merrill Company Inc., by Hallmark, $25.00–30.00. Right: **Raggedy Ann and Andy cookie cutters,** 4", 2-piece plastic, ©1987 Macmillan Inc., by Wecolite Co., Inc., $8.00–10.00 each.

Raggedy Ann, Raggedy Andy, and Raggedy Arthur rubber figurines, 2" to 2½", ©1981 Bobbs-Merrill Co. Inc., by W. Berrie, $6.00–8.00 each.

193

Left: **Raggedy Ann and Andy mug,** 4", plastic, ©1977 Bobbs-Merrill Co. Inc., $6.00–8.00. Right: **Raggedy Ann and Andy glass holder with candle,** 2½" tall, Hallmark, ©1975 Bobbs-Merrill Co. Inc., $15.00–18.00.

Left: **Raggedy Ann and Andy ceramic dish,** 3½" diameter, "Ask grandma/grandpa" design, $4.00–6.00. Right: **Raggedy Ann and Andy ceramic dish,** 8" diameter, "Sunday's child" design, $8.00–12.00.

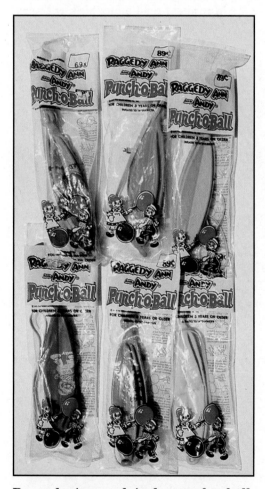

Raggedy Ann and Andy punch-o-ball, 14" diameter inflated, ©1972 Bobbs-Merrill Co. Inc., by Oak Rubber Co., $15.00–20.00 each.

Left: **Raggedy Ann bendee doll,** 6" tall, rubber, ©1978 Bobbs-Merrill Co. Inc., by Amscan Inc., $10.00–12.00. Center: **Raggedy Ann bendee doll,** 2½", rubber, ©1968 Bobbs-Merrill Co. Inc., Hong Kong, $12.00–15.00. Right: **Raggedy Andy bendee doll,** 6" tall, rubber, ©1978 Bobbs-Merrill Co. Inc., by Amscan Inc., $10.00–12.00.

Plastic picture frame, 8" x 10", shows a girl holding Raggedy Andy doll, $5.00–8.00.

Raggedy Ann and Andy ceramic tile in wrought iron holder, 11½", $18.00–22.00.

Raggedy Ann and Andy Super Service, plastic, four spoons, four forks, ©Bobbs-Merrill Co. Inc., by Hallmark, $15.00–18.00.

Raggedy Ann and Andy decals, 5" square, ©1974 Bobbs-Merrill Co. Inc., by Hallmark #50HD143-9, $15.00–18.00 pair.

Raggedy Ann and Andy McDonald's Happy Meal box, ©1989 Macmillan Inc., $12.00–15.00.

Left: **Raggedy Ann and Andy three dimensional stickers,** vinyl, ©1978 Bobbs-Merrill Co. Inc., $10.00–12.00. Right: **Raggedy Ann and Andy puffy stickers,** vinyl, ©1986 Bobbs-Merrill Co. Inc., by Larami, $10.00–12.00.

Raggedy Ann and Andy plastic figurines with play house, figurines approx. 2½", ©1988 Macmillan Inc., $8.00–10.00 each.

Raggedy Andy plastic figurines with play house, figurines approx. 2½", camel is 3¼", ©1988 Macmillan Inc., $8.00–10.00 each.

Raggedy Ann, Raggedy Andy, and Raggedy Arthur dolls, plastic and rubber, dolls are 4", dog is 2½", ©1980 Bobbs-Merrill Co. Inc., $15.00–18.00 set.

Raggedy Ann, Raggedy Andy, and Raggedy Arthur dolls, rubber/vinyl, yarn hair, ©Bobbs-Merrill Co. Inc., by Janex, $20.00–25.00.

Left to right: **Raggedy Ann rubber doll,** 3¾", ©Knickerbocker Toy Co. Inc., $8.00–10.00. **Raggedy Ann rubber doll,** 4½", $8.00–10.00. **Raggedy Ann and Andy plastic figurines,** 3", ©Diener Ind., probably some sort of promotional item, like from cereal, $3.00–6.00. **Raggedy Andy doll,** 4", vinyl and rubber, $4.00–6.00.

Little Raggedys room decorations, self-adhesive decorations, ©1991 Macmillan Inc., by Priss Prints Inc., $22.00–25.00.

Raggedy Ann and Andy dolls on springs, 6", made of stryofoam and cloth, spring attaches to ropes at top and you use to hang from ceiling, probably above child's bed, they go up an down on their spring, ©1973 Bobbs-Merrill Co. Inc., unusual, $45.00–55.00 set.

Raggedy Ann mini vanity, plastic with mirror and trinket drawer, 3¼", has box, ©1978, 1981 Bobbs-Merrill Co. Inc., by Pussy Willow Creations, $16.00–18.00.

Left: **Raggedy Ann and Andy A Musical Adventure video tape,** ©1977 Character Licensing Inc, ©1985 CBS/FOX Co., $12.00–15.00. Right: **Soundtrack 8-track tape,** from the movie, *Raggedy Ann and Andy A Musical Adventure,* ©1977 CBS Inc., $6.00–8.00.

Raggedy Ann and Andy driftwood type wall plaque, 12½", ©1974 DAL "Nifty Drifty," $8.00–12.00.

Raggedy Ann and Andy teapot, 2", ceramic, from tea set, $2.00–3.00.

Raggedy Ann and Andy electric feeding dish, plastic, ©1978 Bobbs-Merrill Co. Inc., by Nursery Needs, $15.00–18.00.

Raggedy Ann and Andy musical mobile, ©1980 Bobbs-Merrill Co. Inc., by Dolly Toy, $20.00–25.00.

Raggedy Ann and Andy baby bib, 13" x 10", terry cloth with vinyl back, $14.00–18.00.

Raggedy Ann needle holder, 5", paper, Japan, $12.00–15.00.

Raggedy Ann and Andy pet rocks, 2" to 2½", ©1969 B. Atkinson, $15.00–18.00 each.

Raggedy Ann and Andy puffy prints, 7½" x 9½", ©1942 J.G. Co. & Georgene Novelties Inc., Third Dimension Picture, $35.00–45.00 each.

Raggedy Ann and Andy candles, 5", paper sticker "fine quality Lego Japan," $12.00–15 pair.

Raggedy Ann and Andy puffy print, 7½" x 9½", ©1942 J.G. Co. & Georgene Novelties Inc., Third Dimension Picture, $35.00–45.00

Raggedy Ann and Andy candles, 5½", paper sticker "Japan," $12.00–15.00 pair.

Raggedy Ann and Andy magnets, 7", vinyl, ©1978 Bobbs-Merrill Co. Inc., $10.00–12.00 set.

Raggedy Ann and Andy ball, vinyl, inflatable to 20", ©1974 Bobbs-Merrill Co. Inc., by Ideal, $30.00–35.00.

Raggedy Ann and Andy Meyercord decorator decals, 8½" x 13½", $8.00–10.00.

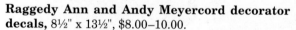

Raggedy Ann and Andy prints, 9" x 11", ©1973 Prints Charming, De'Leon Art Co., $5.00–6.00 each.

Raggedy Ann and Andy combination magnets/stickers, 17" x 12½", set of 48 vinyl magnets on original metal store display, ©1978 Bobbs-Merrill Co. Inc., $55.00–65.00.

Raggedy Ann and Andy figurines, 5½", papier mache, made in Taiwan, $8.00–12.00 pair.

Raggedy Ann wall bag, vinyl with four pockets, ©1981 Bobbs-Merrill Co. Inc., by Pussy Willow Creations, No. 81/1, $10.00–15.00.

Raggedy Ann and Andy tin, 8½" x 10" round, metal, ©1988 Macmillan Inc., $25.00–30.00.

Raggedy Ann and Andy cookie tin, 3¼" tall, 9¾" round, metal, ©1987 Macmillan Inc., by Parco Foods, $20.00–25.00.

Left: **Raggedy Ann and Andy popcorn tin,** 14" tall, 12" round, metal, ©1988 Macmillan Inc., $30.00–35.00. Right: **Raggedy Ann and Andy tin,** 7" x 6½" round, metal, resembles paint can, ©1988 Macmillan Inc., $15.00–18.00.

Left: **Raggedy Ann and Andy tin,** 3" x 5" round, ©1988 Macmillan Inc., by The Tin Box Company of America Inc., $8.00–10.00. Right: **Raggedy Ann and Andy sand pail,** 8", metal, ©1971 Bobbs-Merrill Co. Inc., by Chein Playthings, $35.00–40.00.

Raggedy Ann and Andy chocolate candies, 3½", by Sarris Candies, $3.00–5.00 each.

Raggedy Ann cake mold, 9½", two-piece aluminum, ©1973 Wilton, $20.00–25.00.

Raggedy Ann and Andy linen prints, 7½" x 9½", ©1975 Bobbs-Merrill Co. Inc., $18.00–22.00.

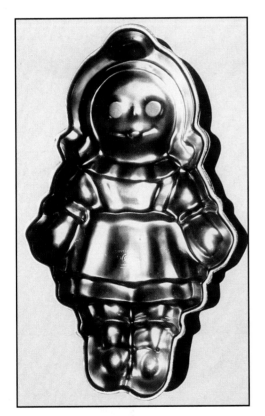

Raggedy Ann cake pan, 17", aluminum, by Wilton ©1971, $12.00–15.00.

Raggedy Ann and Andy 3-D print, 9" x 11", paper in yellow wood frame, marked Ellen Werxheim 77, $18.00–22.00.

Raggedy Ann and Andy wall plaques, approx. 5½" square, chalkware, by Miller Studio Inc., $30.00–35.00.

Raggedy Ann and Andy wall plaques, 12", ceramic, $20.00–25.00 each.

Raggedy Ann wall plaque, 14" long, wooden with painted-on design, marked "A.W.," $15.00–18.00.

Raggedy Ann and Andy wall plaque, 10" tall, plastic, ©1977 Bobbs-Merrill Co. Inc., by Dart Industries, $20.00–25.00.

Marionette-type Raggedy Ann and Andy dolls, 9½", wooden, arms and legs move, made in Western Germany, $35.00–40.00 each.

Raggedy Ann and Andy boxed play set, A Golden Take-Along, includes two Little Golden books; two Tell-A-Tale books, one Golden Shape book, and finger puppets, ©1977 Bobbs-Merrill Co. Inc., by Western Publishing Corp Inc., $35.00–40.00.

Raggedy Ann ball and jack set, by Hallmark #89PF140-9, $18.00–22.00.

Raggedy Ann and Andy crayon box, 4½" tall, metal, ©1974 Bobbs-Merrill Co. Inc., by Chein, $18.00–22.00.

Left: **Raggedy Ann, Raggedy Andy, and Camel dish,** 8½", ceramic, ©1941 Johnny Gruelle Co., by Crooksville, $45.00–50.00. Right: **Raggedy Ann, Raggedy Andy, and Uncle Clem bowl,** 5¼", ceramic, ©1941 Johnny Gruelle Co., by Crooksville, $30.00–35.00. Condition shown is worth about $15.00.

Left: **Raggedy Ann, Raggedy Andy, and Uncle Clem dish,** 7", ceramic, ©1941 Johnny Gruelle Co., by Crooksville, $35.00–40.00. Right: **Raggedy Ann, Raggedy Andy, and Uncle Clem divided dish,** 7¾", ceramic, ©1941 Johnny Gruelle Co., by Crooksville, $45.00–50.00.

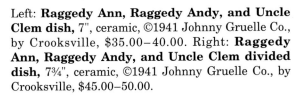

205

Raggedy Ann and Andy musical mug, 4" tall, ceramic, wind-up, plays music when mug is lifted, ©1971 Bobbs-Merrill Co. Inc., by Schmid, $30.00–35.00.

Raggedy Andy musical mug, 4" tall, ceramic, wind-up, plays music when mug is lifted, ©1971 Bobbs-Merrill Co. Inc., by Schmid, $30.00–35.00.

Raggedy Ann and Andy water globe, 6" tall, musical, by Dept. 56 Inc., $25.00–30.00.

MUSIC BOXES

Raggedy Ann music box, 6", made of carved wood, cloth clothing, moveable arms, legs, and head, ©1971 Bobbs-Merrill Co., Inc., made in Italy by ANRI, paper label: Reuge, "Talk to the Animals" Swiss musical movement, $55.00–65.00.

Raggedy Andy music box, 6", made of carved wood, cloth clothing, moveable arms, legs, and head, ©1971 Bobbs-Merrill Co., Inc., made in Italy by ANRI paper label: Reuge, "When The Saints Go Marching In" Swiss musical movement, $55.00–65.00.

Left: **Raggedy Ann and Andy music box,** 7", ceramic, seesaw moves up and down and box rotates while playing, paper label: "Japan," $15.00–18.00. Right: **Raggedy Ann and Andy music box,** 7½", ceramic, plays the *Theme from Love Story,* marked "Japan" on plastic base, $15.00–20.00.

Left: **Raggedy Ann and Andy music box,** 6", ceramic, plays "School Days," marked Japan, $15.00–20.00. Right: **Raggedy Ann music box,** 6½", ceramic, has paper Schmid hang tag, paper label: Schmid, No. 254, Japan, tune: *The Entertainer,* ©1981 Bobbs-Merrill Co., Inc., Schmid, hand painted, $35.00–40.00.

Raggedy Ann music box, ceramic, 5½", has paper Schmid hang tag, paper label: Schmid, No. 349, Japan, tune: *Windmills of Your Mind.* ©1981 Bobbs-Merrill Co., Inc., Schmid, hand painted, $35.00–40.00.

Raggedy Andy music box, 6½", ceramic, has paper Schmid hang tag, paper label: Schmid, No. 105, Japan, tune: *Yesterday.* ©1981 Bobbs-Merrill Co., Inc., Schmid, hand painted, $35.00–40.00.

Left: **Raggedy Ann and Andy music box,** 6¾", ceramic, has "School Days, School Days, Dear Old Golden Rule Days" written across front, plays *School Days,* by Chadwick-Miller, ©1972 Japan, $20.00–25.00. Right: **Raggedy Ann and Andy music box,** 6½", ceramic, Andy holds a balloon (ceramic) on a wire, plays *Hello Dolly,* paper label: ©1972 Fitz and Floyd, Inc., $25.00–30.00.

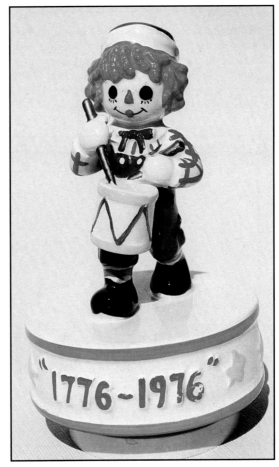

Raggedy Ann and Andy Bicentennial "1776 – 1976" music boxes, 6", ceramic, ©1975 Bobbs-Merrill Co., Inc., Raggedy Ann sewing American flag and plays tune no. 256, *You're a Grand Old Flag,* Raggedy Andy playing drum and tune no. 146, *Yankee Doodle,* paper labels: Schmid Bros. Inc., Made in Japan, $30.00–35.00 each.

Raggedy Ann music box, 6½", ceramic, Ann should be holding something in her outstretched hand, but piece is missing, paper label: Schmid Bros. Inc., Tune No. 201, *Theme from Love Story,* Made in Japan, ©1973 Bobbs-Merrill Co., Inc., $22.00–25.00.

Raggedy Andy music box, 4¼", ceramic, paper label: Schmid Bros. Inc., Tune No. 144, *King of the Road,* Made in Japan, ©1974 Bobbs-Merrill Co. Inc., $18.00–20.00.

Raggedy Ann and Andy music box, 5", wooden with decal design, hangs on wall, pull string to wind and play music, plays *Close to You,* ©1972 Bobbs-Merrill Co., Inc., $25.00–30.00.

Raggedy Ann Santa music box, 7¼", ceramic, plays *Twelve Days of Christmas,* paper label: Berman & Anderson, Inc., made in Japan, $22.00–25.00.

Left: **Raggedy Ann music box,** 8½", ceramic, paper Schmid hang tag, plays *School Days,* ©1971 Bobbs-Merrill Co., Inc., Schmid, Japan, $35.00–40.00. Right: **Raggedy Andy music box,** 8½", ceramic, paper label: Schmid Bros. Inc., Tune 199 *Do-Re-Mi,* made in Japan, ©1971 Bobbs-Merrill Co., Inc., $35.00–40.00.

Raggedy Ann and Andy music box, wooden, plays *It's a Small World,* by The American Music Box Co., $12.00–16.00.

Raggedy Ann and Andy music box, 6", wood, ceramic, and plastic, brass plate on front of base engraved "Raggedy Ann and Andy," figurines rotate when music plays, was available only in Japan, ©1993 Macmillian, Inc., paper label: Tune *It's a Small World,* $45.00–55.00.

Raggedy Ann and Andy music box, 8½", made of cloth and styrofoam, paper label: Schmid Bros., Inc, Tune No. 201, *Theme from Love Story* made in Japan, ©1972 Bobbs-Merrill Co., Inc., $28.00–32.00.

PAPER ITEMS

Raggedy Ann and Andy fold over cards, 13" x 6½", eight in pack with stickers, ©1990 Macmillan Inc., by Creative Learning Products Inc.; top: invitations; center: birthday cards; bottom: thank you notes; $10.00–12.00 each.

Raggedy Ann and Andy miniature playing cards, 2½", ©1974 Bobbs-Merrill Co. Inc., by Hallmark Cards Inc., $12.00–15.00 each.

Raggedy Ann and Andy Letters and Numbers activity placemats, 11" x 17", 24 paper placemats with four crayons, ©1990 Macmillan Inc., by Creative Learning Products Inc., $8.00–10.00.

Raggedy Ann and Andy Activities placemats, 11" x 17", 24 paper placemats with four crayons, ©1990 Macmillan Inc., by Creative Learning Products Inc., $8.00–10.00.

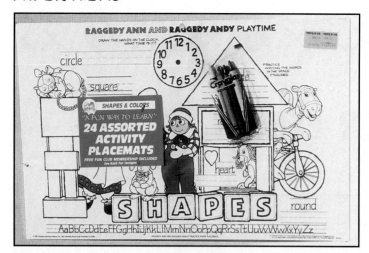

Raggedy Ann and Andy Shapes and Colors activity place-mats, 11" x 17", 24 paper placemats with four crayons, ©1990 Macmillan Inc., by Creative Learning Products Inc., $8.00–10.00.

Left: **Raggedy Ann and Andy notepad,** 3" x 5", ©1975 Bobbs-Merrill Co. Inc., by Plymouth Inc.; center: **Raggedy Ann and Andy notepad,** 3" x 5", by Expression; right: **Raggedy Ann notepad,** 3" x 5", ©1975 Bobbs-Merrill Co. Inc., by Plymouth Inc.; $5.00–8.00 each.

Raggedy Ann and Andy birth announcements, pack of eight, by Hallmark, circa 1980s, $10.00–12.00 each.

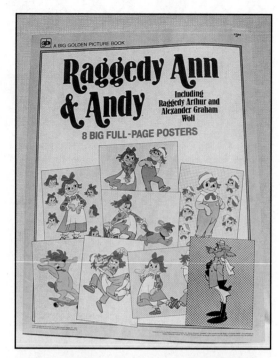

Raggedy Ann and Andy 8 big full-page posters, 20" x 15½", A Big Golden Picture Book, ©1979 Bobbs-Merrill Co. Inc., $25.00–30.00.

Raggedy Ann stationary, 4" x 5½" folded sheets, by Hallmark, #125ST429-1, $12.00–15.00.

Raggedy Ann stationary, boxed set, ©1976 Bobbs-Merrill Co. Inc., by Hallmark, #250ST478-6, $20.00–25.00.

Raggedy Ann stationary, boxed set, ©1974 Bobbs-Merrill Co. Inc., by Hallmark, #250ST126-4, $20.00–25.00.

Left: **Raggedy Ann and Andy postcards,** 3½" x 5½", pack of 24, by Red Farm Studio, $12.00–15.00. Right: **Raggedy Ann and Andy note cards,** 5" x 4", pack of 10 notes and envelopes, $10.00–12.00.

Raggedy Ann "Lap Pack," 20 writing sheets and 10 envelopes all contained in cardboard folder, ©1975 Bobbs-Merrill Co. Inc., by Hallmark, #200BM569-5, $20.00–25.00.

Raggedy Ann and Andy mini coloring book, 6¼" tall, ©1974 Bobbs-Merrill Co. Inc., by Hallmark, #75PF1440-1, $8.00–12.00.

Raggedy Ann and Andy notebooks, 4" x 4¾", spiral binding, available only in Japan, ©1994 Macmillan Inc., by Lyric, $18.00–20.00 each.

Raggedy Ann and Andy notebooks, 6¾" x 7¼", spiral binding, available only in Japan, ©1994 Macmillan Inc., by Lyric, $25.00–30.00 each.

Left: **Raggedy Ann and Andy writing paper,** 6¼" x 7¾", four different illustrations, available only in Japan, ©1994 Macmillan Inc., by Lyric, $15.00–18.00. Right: **Raggedy Ann and Andy envelopes,** ten of Ann, ten of Andy, available only in Japan, ©1994 Macmillan Inc., by Lyric, $12.00–15.00.

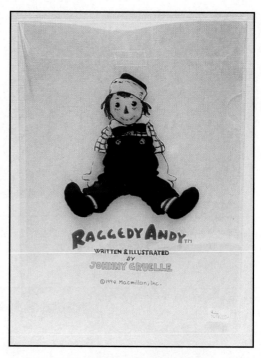

Raggedy Andy book report cover, 8½" x 12", plastic, available only in Japan, ©1994 Macmillan Inc., $18.00–20.00.

Raggedy Ann and Andy movie poster, 28" x 40", ©1977, 1978 Bobbs-Merrill Co. Inc., $20.00–25.00.

216

Raggedy Ann and Raggedy Andy stationary set, includes writing paper, stickers, and envelopes, available only in Japan, ©1992 Macmillan Inc., by Lyric, $15.00–18.00 each.

Left: **Raggedy Ann and Andy self-adhesive stickers,** 6" tall, pack of 3, ©Bobbs-Merrill Co. Inc., by Hallmark, $12.00–15.00. Right: **Raggedy Andy paper bookplates,** 2¾" x 3¾", 50 in box, ©Bobbs-Merrill Co. Inc., by Hallmark, #150HBM28-1, $8.00–12.00.

Raggedy Ann and Raggedy Andy stationary, ten sheets of paper, ten shaped sheets, ten envelopes, available only in Japan, ©1994 Macmillan Inc., by Lyric, $15.00–18.00 each.

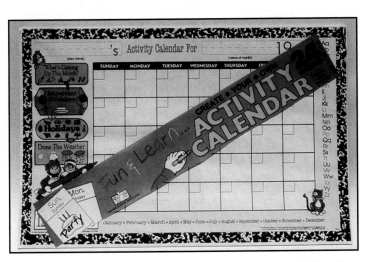

Raggedy Ann and Andy Fun & Learn Activity Calendar, 11" x 17", ©1990 Macmillan Inc., by Creative Learning Products, Inc., $20.00–22.00.

Raggedy Ann sewing cards, 8" x 6", pack of four party favors, ©Bobbs-Merrill Company Inc., by Hallmark #59PF140-5, $15.00–20.00.

217

Instructional books, both are ©1978–1984 Bobbs-Merrill Co. Inc., by Gaylemot Publishing Co., Inc., $10.00–12.00 each. Left: *Raggedy Ann and Andy Quilting,* #GM-501; right: *Raggedy Ann and Andy Stenciling,* #GM-504.

Instructional books, both are ©1978–1984 Bobbs-Merrill Co. Inc., by Gaylemot Publishing Co., Inc., $10.00–12.00 each. Left: *Raggedy Ann and Andy Bread Dough,* #GM-505; right: *Raggedy Ann and Andy Parties and Playmates,* #GM-506.

Raggedy Andy Fabric Finish advertisement, ©1968 Faultless Starch Company, $8.00–12.00.

Left: **Raggedy Ann and Andy stickers,** eight sheets, ©1990 Macmillan Inc., by Hallmark, $8.00–10.00. Center: **Raggedy Ann and Andy stickers,** four sheets of self-adhesive stickers, ©1980 Bobbs-Merrill Co. Inc., by Ambassador, $8.00–10.00. Right: **Raggedy Ann and Andy seals,** 48 self-adhesive seals, ©1969 Bobbs-Merrill Co. Inc., by Hallmark, $18.00–20.00.

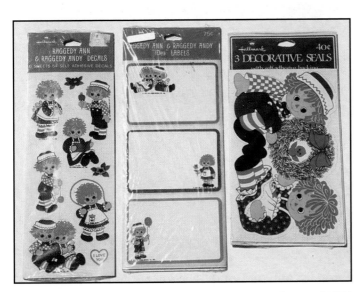

Left: **Raggedy Ann and Andy stickers,** six sheets, ©1974 Bobbs-Merrill Co. Inc., by Hallmark, $8.00–10.00. Center: **Raggedy Ann and Andy "IDea" labels,** six sheets, ©1974 Bobbs-Merrill Co. Inc., by Hallmark, #75QG1191, $8.00–12.00. Right: **Raggedy Ann and Andy decorative seals,** 6" x 3¾", ©Hallmark, $10.00–14.00.

Raggedy Ann and Andy notepaper holders, 9" tall, cardboard, 40 sheets of paper, ©Bobbs-Merrill Company Inc., by Hallmark, Raggedy Ann #60ST992, Raggedy Andy #60ST993, $15.00–18.00 each.

Raggedy Ann and Andy mobile, 13½", cardboard, legs and heads attached with string for movement, by Hallmark, $25.00–35.00 each.

Raggedy Ann and Andy cube mobile, cardboard, ©1974 Bobbs-Merrill Co. Inc., by Hallmark, #125HD143-8, $20.00–25.00.

Raggedy Ann and Andy playing cards, 2" x 3½", ©1975 Bobbs-Merrill Co. Inc., by Hallmark, $12.00–15.00 each. Top row, left to right: "Witch Switch," "Willy Wiggle," "Hide and Go Peek"; bottom row: "Magic Pebble" and "Raggedy Rummy."

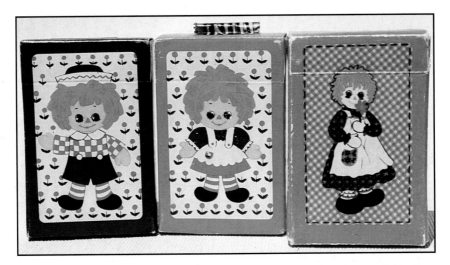

Left: **Raggedy Andy playing cards,** 2½" x 1½", ©The Bobbs-Merrill Co. Inc.,
Hallmark #75BC140-6; center: **Raggedy Ann playing cards,** 2½" x 1½",
©The Bobbs-Merrill Co. Inc., Hallmark #75BC140-5; right: **Raggedy Ann
playing cards,** 2½" x 1½", ©The Bobbs-Merrill Co. Inc., Hallmark
#75BC760-2; $10.00–12.00 each.

Doll Design Magazine, Oct/Nov 90, $8.00–10.00.

Good Housekeeping magazine, December
1971, has Raggedy Ann and Andy cookie recipe,
$10.00–15.00.

"Raggedy Ann I Love You" music, from the
1941 Paramount Pictures technicolor cartoon,
Raggedy Ann and Raggedy Andy, $15.00–20.00.

Raggedy Ann and Andy Home Decoration Book,
9" x 13", press-out designs, ©Bobbs-Merrill Company
Inc., by Hallmark, $20.00–25.00.

Advertisement, for Raggedy Ann and Andy melmac dishes, order dolls shown on back of form for
$6.95, $10.00–12.00.

Advertisement, for ordering 4 full-color art
prints of the Raggedys, $3.00–5.00.

Advertisement, for Raggedy Ann and Andy and the Camel with the Wrinkled Knees, ©1977 KTC, $12.00–15.00.

Advertisement, for Knickerbocker Raggedy Ann, ©1981 KTC, $10.00–12.00.

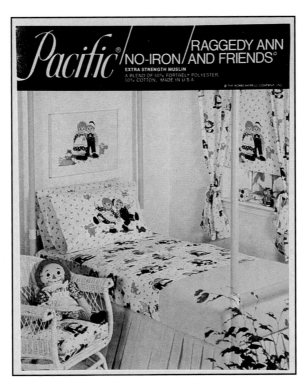

Advertisement, for Pacific bedroom accessories, $8.00–10.00.

Raggedy Ann portfolio, cardboard, ©1975 Bobbs-Merrill Co. Inc., by Plymouth Inc., $12.00–15.00.

Raggedy Ann and Andy poster, 21½" x 27", ©1970 Bobbs-Merrill Co. Inc., by Determined Productions, $10.00–15.00.

PLANTERS & VASES

Raggedy Ann and Andy planter, 3¾", ceramic, ©1976 Bobbs-Merrill Co. Inc., by Rubens Originals, photo on right shows back decal, this same decal appears on the back of each Rubens Originals, $15.00–20.00.

Raggedy Ann and Andy watering can, 4¼", ceramic, ©1976 Bobbs-Merrill Co. Inc., by Rubens Originals, $15.00–20.00.

Raggedy Ann and Andy watering can, 4¼", ceramic, ©1976 Bobbs-Merrill Co. Inc., by Rubens Originals, $15.00–20.00.

Raggedy Ann and Andy watering can, 4¼", ceramic, ©1976 Bobbs-Merrill Co. Inc., by Rubens Originals, $15.00–20.00.

Raggedy Ann and Andy watering can, 4¼", ceramic, ©1976 Bobbs-Merrill Co. Inc., by Rubens Originals, $15.00–20.00.

Raggedy Ann and Andy planter, 3¼" x 6½", ceramic, ©1976 Bobbs-Merrill Co. Inc., by Rubens Originals, $15.00–20.00.

Raggedy Ann and Andy planter, 3¼" x 6½", ceramic, ©1976 Bobbs-Merrill Co. Inc., by Rubens Originals, $15.00–20.00.

Raggedy Ann and Andy cups, 4¾", ceramic, ©1976 Bobbs-Merrill Co. Inc., by Rubens Originals, $15.00–20.00 each.

Raggedy Ann and Andy mug, 4", ceramic, ©1976 Bobbs-Merrill Co. Inc., by Rubens Originals, $15.00–20.00.

Raggedy Ann and Andy vases, 6½" tall, plastic, stamped "Rubens Originals L.A. 1980," $10.00–15.00 each.

Raggedy Ann and Andy planters, 3½" tall, plastic, stamped "Rubens Originals L.A. 1980," $10.00–15.00 each.

ABOUT THE AUTHOR

Kim Avery has been collecting Raggedy Ann and Andy dolls and related items for over ten years. As her collection grew, she realized that there was a need for information on the many different Raggedy Ann and Andy items, so she decided to write a book based on the vast array of collectibles she owns.

Kim is a resident in Southern California and works as an office automation assistant. In her leisure time, she searches antique stores, garage sales, and doll shows for new treasures for her collection.

Kim enjoys meeting fellow collectors and sharing Raggedy Ann and Andy information. She can be contacted via e-mail at CyberRagdy@aol.com.

Kim Avery with her buddy, Raggedy Andy.

This is a partial view of Kim's vast Raggedy Ann and Andy collection.

COLLECTOR BOOKS

Informing Today's Collector

For over two decades we have been keeping collectors informed on trends and values in all fields of antiques and collectibles.

DOLLS, FIGURES & TEDDY BEARS

4707	A Decade of **Barbie** Dolls & Collectibles, 1981–1991, Summers	$19.95
4631	**Barbie** Doll Boom, 1986–1995, Augustyniak	$18.95
2079	**Barbie** Doll Fashions, Volume I, Eames	$24.95
3957	**Barbie** Exclusives, Rana	$18.95
4632	**Barbie** Exclusives, Book II, Rana	$18.95
4557	**Barbie,** The First 30 Years, Deutsch	$24.95
4657	**Barbie** Years, 1959–1995, Olds	$16.95
3310	**Black Dolls,** 1820–1991, Perkins	$17.95
3873	**Black Dolls,** Book II, Perkins	$17.95
1529	Collector's Encyclopedia of **Barbie** Dolls, DeWein	$19.95
4506	Collector's Guide to **Dolls in Uniform,** Bourgeois	$18.95
3727	Collector's Guide to **Ideal Dolls,** Izen	$18.95
3728	Collector's Guide to Miniature **Teddy Bears,** Powell	$17.95
3967	Collector's Guide to **Trolls,** Peterson	$19.95
4571	**Liddle Kiddles,** Identification & Value Guide, Langford	$18.95
4645	**Madame Alexander** Dolls Price Guide #21, Smith	$9.95
3733	**Modern Collector's** Dolls, Sixth Series, Smith	$24.95
3991	**Modern Collector's** Dolls, Seventh Series, Smith	$24.95
4647	**Modern Collector's** Dolls, Eighth Series, Smith	$24.95
4640	Patricia Smith's **Doll Values,** Antique to Modern, 12th Edition	$12.95
3826	Story of **Barbie,** Westenhouser	$19.95
1513	**Teddy Bears & Steiff** Animals, Mandel	$9.95
1817	**Teddy Bears & Steiff** Animals, 2nd Series, Mandel	$19.95
2084	**Teddy Bears, Annalee's & Steiff** Animals, 3rd Series, Mandel	$19.95
1808	Wonder of **Barbie,** Manos	$9.95
1430	World of **Barbie** Dolls, Manos	$9.95

FURNITURE

1457	American **Oak** Furniture, McNerney	$9.95
3716	American **Oak** Furniture, Book II, McNerney	$12.95
1118	Antique **Oak** Furniture, Hill	$7.95
2132	Collector's Encyclopedia of **American** Furniture, Vol. I, Swedberg	$24.95
2271	Collector's Encyclopedia of **American** Furniture, Vol. II, Swedberg	$24.95
3720	Collector's Encyclopedia of **American** Furniture, Vol. III, Swedberg	$24.95
3878	Collector's Guide to **Oak** Furniture, George	$12.95
1755	Furniture of the **Depression Era,** Swedberg	$19.95
3906	**Heywood-Wakefield** Modern Furniture, Rouland	$18.95
1885	**Victorian** Furniture, Our American Heritage, McNerney	$9.95
3829	**Victorian** Furniture, Our American Heritage, Book II, McNerney	$9.95
3869	**Victorian** Furniture books, 2 volume set, McNerney	$19.90

JEWELRY, HATPINS, WATCHES & PURSES

1712	Antique & Collector's **Thimbles** & Accessories, Mathis	$19.95
1748	Antique **Purses,** Revised Second Ed., Holiner	$19.95
1278	Art Nouveau & Art Deco **Jewelry,** Baker	$9.95
4558	**Christmas Pins,** Past and Present, Gallina	$18.95
3875	Collecting Antique **Stickpins,** Kerins	$16.95
3722	Collector's Ency. of **Compacts, Carryalls & Face Powder Boxes,** Mueller	$24.95
4655	Complete Price Guide to **Watches,** #16, Shugart	$26.95
1716	Fifty Years of Collectible **Fashion Jewelry,** 1925-1975, Baker	$19.95
1424	**Hatpins** & Hatpin Holders, Baker	$9.95
4570	Ladies' **Compacts,** Gerson	$24.95
1181	100 Years of Collectible **Jewelry,** 1850-1950, Baker	$9.95
2348	20th Century Fashionable Plastic **Jewelry,** Baker	$19.95
3830	Vintage **Vanity Bags & Purses,** Gerson	$24.95

TOYS, MARBLES & CHRISTMAS COLLECTIBLES

3427	**Advertising Character** Collectibles, Dotz	$17.95
2333	Antique & Collector's **Marbles,** 3rd Ed., Grist	$9.95
3827	Antique & Collector's **Toys,** 1870–1950, Longest	$24.95
3956	Baby Boomer **Games,** Identification & Value Guide, Polizzi	$24.95
3717	**Christmas** Collectibles, 2nd Edition, Whitmyer	$24.95
1752	**Christmas** Ornaments, Lights & Decorations, Johnson	$19.95
4649	Classic Plastic **Model Kits,** Polizzi	$24.95

4559	Collectible **Action Figures,** 2nd Ed., Manos	$17.95
3874	Collectible Coca-Cola Toy **Trucks,** deCourtivron	$24.95
2338	Collector's Encyclopedia of **Disneyana,** Longest, Stern	$24.95
4639	Collector's Guide to **Diecast Toys & Scale Models,** Johnson	$19.95
4651	Collector's Guide to **Tinker Toys,** Strange	$18.95
4566	Collector's Guide to **Tootsietoys,** 2nd Ed., Richter	$19.95
3436	Grist's Big Book of **Marbles**	$19.95
3970	Grist's Machine-Made & Contemporary **Marbles,** 2nd Ed.	$9.95
4569	**Howdy Doody,** Collector's Reference and Trivia Guide, Koch	$16.95
4723	**Matchbox®** Toys, 1948 to 1993, Johnson, 2nd Ed.	$18.95
3823	**Mego** Toys, An Illustrated Value Guide, Chrouch	15.95
1540	**Modern Toys** 1930–1980, Baker	$19.95
3888	**Motorcycle** Toys, Antique & Contemporary, Gentry/Downs	$18.95
4728	Schroeder's Collectible **Toys,** Antique to Modern Price Guide, 3rd Ed.	$17.95
1886	Stern's Guide to **Disney** Collectibles	$14.95
2139	Stern's Guide to **Disney** Collectibles, 2nd Series	$14.95
3975	Stern's Guide to **Disney** Collectibles, 3rd Series	$18.95
2028	**Toys,** Antique & Collectible, Longest	$14.95
3979	**Zany Characters** of the Ad World, Lamphier	$16.95

INDIANS, GUNS, KNIVES, TOOLS, PRIMITIVES

1868	Antique **Tools,** Our American Heritage, McNerney	$9.95
2015	Archaic **Indian** Points & Knives, Edler	$14.95
1426	**Arrowheads** & Projectile Points, Hothem	$7.95
4633	**Big Little Books,** Jacobs	$18.95
2279	**Indian** Artifacts of the Midwest, Hothem	$14.95
3885	**Indian** Artifacts of the Midwest, Book II, Hothem	$16.95
1964	**Indian** Axes & Related Stone Artifacts, Hothem	$14.95
2023	**Keen Kutter** Collectibles, Heuring	$14.95
4724	Modern **Guns,** Identification & Values, 11th Ed., Quertermous	$12.95
4505	Standard Guide to **Razors,** Ritchie & Stewart	$9.95
4730	Standard **Knife** Collector's Guide, 3rd Ed., Ritchie & Stewart	$12.95

PAPER COLLECTIBLES & BOOKS

4633	**Big Little Books,** Jacobs	$18.95
1441	Collector's Guide to **Post Cards,** Wood	$9.95
2081	Guide to Collecting **Cookbooks,** Allen	$14.95
4648	Huxford's **Old Book** Value Guide, 8th Ed.	$19.95
2080	Price Guide to **Cookbooks & Recipe Leaflets,** Dickinson	$9.95
2346	**Sheet Music** Reference & Price Guide, 2nd Ed., Pafik & Guiheen	$18.95
4654	**Victorian Trading Cards,** Historical Reference & Value Guide, Cheadle	$19.95

GLASSWARE

1006	**Cambridge Glass** Reprint 1930–1934	$14.95
1007	**Cambridge Glass** Reprint 1949–1953	$14.95
4561	Collectible **Drinking Glasses,** Chase & Kelly	$17.95
4642	Collectible **Glass Shoes,** Wheatley	$19.95
4553	Coll. **Glassware** from the 40's, 50's & 60's, 3rd Ed., Florence	$19.95
2352	Collector's Encyclopedia of **Akro Agate Glassware,** Florence	$14.95
1810	Collector's Encyclopedia of **American Art Glass,** Shuman	$29.95
3312	Collector's Encyclopedia of **Children's Dishes,** Whitmyer	$19.95
4552	Collector's Encyclopedia of **Depression Glass,** 12th Ed., Florence	$19.95
1664	Collector's Encyclopedia of **Heisey Glass,** 1925–1938, Bredehoft	$24.95
3905	Collector's Encyclopedia of **Milk Glass,** Newbound	$24.95
1523	Colors In **Cambridge Glass,** National Cambridge Society	$19.95
4564	**Crackle Glass,** Weitman	$19.95
2275	**Czechoslovakian Glass** and Collectibles, Barta/Rose	$16.95
4714	**Czechoslovakian Glass** and Collectibles, Book II, Barta/Rose	$16.95
4716	**Elegant Glassware** of the Depression Era, 7th Ed., Florence	$19.95
1380	Encyclopedia of **Pattern Glass,** McClain	$12.95
3981	Ever's Standard **Cut Glass** Value Guide	$12.95
4659	**Fenton** Art Glass, 1907–1939, Whitmyer	$24.95
3725	**Fostoria,** Pressed, Blown & Hand Molded Shapes, Kerr	$24.95
3883	**Fostoria Stemware,** The Crystal for America, Long & Seate	$24.95
3318	**Glass Animals** of the Depression Era, Garmon & Spencer	$19.95
4644	**Imperial Carnival Glass,** Burns	$18.95

COLLECTOR BOOKS
Informing Today's Collector

3886	**Kitchen Glassware** of the Depression Years, 5th Ed., Florence	$19.95
2394	**Oil Lamps II**, Glass Kerosene Lamps, Thuro	$24.95
4725	Pocket Guide to **Depression Glass**, 10th Ed., Florence	$9.95
4634	Standard Encylopedia of **Carnival Glass**, 5th Ed., Edwards	$24.95
4635	Standard **Carnival Glass** Price Guide, 10th Ed.	$9.95
3974	Standard Encylopedia of **Opalescent Glass**, Edwards	$19.95
4731	**Stemware Identification**, Featuring Cordials with Values, Florence	$24.95
3326	**Very Rare Glassware** of the Depression Years, 3rd Series, Florence	$24.95
3909	**Very Rare Glassware** of the Depression Years, 4th Series, Florence	$24.95
4732	**Very Rare Glassware** of the Depression Years, 5th Series, Florence	$24.95
4656	**Westmoreland Glass**, Wilson	$24.95
2224	World of **Salt Shakers**, 2nd Ed., Lechner	$24.95

POTTERY

4630	**American Limoges**, Limoges	$24.95
1312	**Blue & White Stoneware**, McNerney	$9.95
1958	So. Potteries **Blue Ridge Dinnerware**, 3rd Ed., Newbound	$14.95
1959	**Blue Willow**, 2nd Ed., Gaston	$14.95
3816	Collectible **Vernon Kilns**, Nelson	$24.95
3311	Collecting **Yellow Ware** – Id. & Value Guide, McAllister	$16.95
1373	Collector's Encyclopedia of **American Dinnerware**, Cunningham	$24.95
3815	Collector's Encyclopedia of **Blue Ridge Dinnerware**, Newbound	$19.95
4658	Collector's Encyclopedia of **Brush-McCoy Pottery**, Huxford	$24.95
2272	Collector's Encyclopedia of **California Pottery**, Chipman	$24.95
3811	Collector's Encyclopedia of **Colorado Pottery**, Carlton	$24.95
2133	Collector's Encyclopedia of **Cookie Jars**, Roerig	$24.95
3723	Collector's Encyclopedia of **Cookie Jars**, Volume II, Roerig	$24.95
3429	Collector's Encyclopedia of **Cowan Pottery**, Saloff	$24.95
4638	Collector's Encyclopedia of **Dakota Potteries**, Dommel	$24.95
2209	Collector's Encyclopedia of **Fiesta**, 7th Ed., Huxford	$19.95
4718	Collector's Encyclopedia of **Figural Planters & Vases**, Newbound	$19.95
3961	Collector's Encyclopedia of **Early Noritake**, Alden	$24.95
1439	Collector's Encyclopedia of **Flow Blue China**, Gaston	$19.95
3812	Collector's Encyclopedia of **Flow Blue China**, 2nd Ed., Gaston	$24.95
3813	Collector's Encyclopedia of **Hall China**, 2nd Ed., Whitmyer	$24.95
3431	Collector's Encyclopedia of **Homer Laughlin China**, Jasper	$24.95
1276	Collector's Encyclopedia of **Hull Pottery**, Roberts	$19.95
4573	Collector's Encyclopedia of **Knowles, Taylor & Knowles**, Gaston	$24.95
3962	Collector's Encyclopedia of **Lefton China**, DeLozier	$19.95
2210	Collector's Encyclopedia of **Limoges Porcelain**, 2nd Ed., Gaston	$24.95
2334	Collector's Encyclopedia of **Majolica Pottery**, Katz-Marks	$19.95
1358	Collector's Encyclopedia of **McCoy Pottery**, Huxford	$19.95
3963	Collector's Encyclopedia of **Metlox Potteries**, Gibbs Jr.	$24.95
3313	Collector's Encyclopedia of **Niloak**, Gifford	$19.95
3837	Collector's Encyclopedia of **Nippon Porcelain I**, Van Patten	$24.95
2089	Collector's Ency. of **Nippon Porcelain**, 2nd Series, Van Patten	$24.95
1665	Collector's Ency. of **Nippon Porcelain**, 3rd Series, Van Patten	$24.95
3836	**Nippon Porcelain** Price Guide, Van Patten	$9.95
1447	Collector's Encyclopedia of **Noritake**, Van Patten	$19.95
3432	Collector's Encyclopedia of **Noritake**, 2nd Series, Van Patten	$24.95
1037	Collector's Encyclopedia of **Occupied Japan**, Vol. I, Florence	$14.95
1038	Collector's Encyclopedia of **Occupied Japan**, Vol. II, Florence	$14.95
2088	Collector's Encyclopedia of **Occupied Japan**, Vol. III, Florence	$14.95
2019	Collector's Encyclopedia of **Occupied Japan**, Vol. IV, Florence	$14.95
2335	Collector's Encyclopedia of **Occupied Japan**, Vol. V, Florence	$14.95
3964	Collector's Encyclopedia of **Pickard China**, Reed	$24.95
1311	Collector's Encyclopedia of **R.S. Prussia**, 1st Series, Gaston	$24.95
1715	Collector's Encyclopedia of **R.S. Prussia**, 2nd Series, Gaston	$24.95
3726	Collector's Encyclopedia of **R.S. Prussia**, 3rd Series, Gaston	$24.95
3877	Collector's Encyclopedia of **R.S. Prussia**, 4th Series, Gaston	$24.95
1034	Collector's Encyclopedia of **Roseville Pottery**, Huxford	$19.95
1035	Collector's Encyclopedia of **Roseville Pottery**, 2nd Ed., Huxford	$19.95
3357	**Roseville** Price Guide No. 10	$9.95
3965	Collector's Encyclopedia of **Sascha Brastoff**, Conti, Bethany & Seay	$24.95
3314	Collector's Encyclopedia of **Van Briggle** Art Pottery, Sasicki	$24.95
4563	Collector's Encyclopedia of **Wall Pockets**, Newbound	$19.95
2111	Collector's Encyclopedia of **Weller Pottery**, Huxford	$29.95
3452	Coll. Guide to **Country Stoneware & Pottery**, Raycraft	$11.95
2077	Coll. Guide to **Country Stoneware & Pottery**, 2nd Series, Raycraft	$14.95
3434	Coll. Guide to **Hull Pottery**, The Dinnerware Line, Gick-Burke	$16.95

3876	Collector's Guide to **Lu-Ray Pastels**, Meehan	$18.95
3814	Collector's Guide to **Made in Japan** Ceramics, White	$18.95
4646	Collector's Guide to **Made in Japan** Ceramics, Book II, White	$18.95
4565	Collector's Guide to **Rockingham**, The Enduring Ware, Brewer	$14.95
2339	Collector's Guide to **Shawnee Pottery**, Vanderbilt	$19.95
1425	**Cookie Jars**, Westfall	$9.95
3440	**Cookie Jars**, Book II, Westfall	$19.95
3435	Debolt's Dictionary of **American Pottery Marks**	$17.95
2379	Lehner's Ency. of **U.S. Marks** on Pottery, Porcelain & China	$24.95
4722	**McCoy Pottery**, Collector's Reference & Value Guide, Hanson/Nissen	$19.95
3825	**Puritan Pottery**, Morris	$24.95
4726	**Red Wing Art Pottery**, 1920s–1960s, Dollen	$19.95
1670	**Red Wing Collectibles**, DePasquale	$9.95
1440	**Red Wing Stoneware**, DePasquale	$9.95
3738	**Shawnee Pottery**, Mangus	$24.95
4629	Turn of the Century **American Dinnerware**, 1880s–1920s, Jasper	$24.95
4572	**Wall Pockets** of the Past, Perkins	$17.95
3327	**Watt Pottery** – Identification & Value Guide, Morris	$19.95

OTHER COLLECTIBLES

4704	Antique & Collectible **Buttons**, Wisniewski	$19.95
2269	Antique **Brass & Copper** Collectibles, Gaston	$16.95
1880	Antique **Iron**, McNerney	$9.95
3872	Antique **Tins**, Dodge	$24.95
1714	**Black** Collectibles, Gibbs	$19.95
1128	**Bottle** Pricing Guide, 3rd Ed., Cleveland	$7.95
4636	**Celluloid Collectibles**, Dunn	$14.95
3959	**Cereal Box** Bonanza, The 1950's, Bruce	$19.95
3718	Collectible **Aluminum**, Grist	$16.95
3445	Collectible **Cats**, An Identification & Value Guide, Fyke	$18.95
4560	Collectible **Cats**, An Identification & Value Guide, Book II, Fyke	$19.95
1634	Collector's Ency. of Figural & Novelty **Salt & Pepper Shakers**, Davern	$19.95
2020	Collector's Ency. of Figural & Novelty **Salt & Pepper Shakers**, Vol. II, Davern	$19.95
2018	Collector's Encyclopedia of **Granite Ware**, Greguire	$24.95
3430	Collector's Encyclopedia of **Granite Ware**, Book II, Greguire	$24.95
4705	Collector's Guide to **Antique Radios**, 4th Ed., Bunis	$18.95
1916	Collector's Guide to **Art Deco**, Gaston	$14.95
3880	Collector's Guide to **Cigarette Lighters**, Flanagan	$17.95
4637	Collector's Guide to **Cigarette Lighters**, Book II, Flanagan	$17.95
1537	Collector's Guide to **Country Baskets**, Raycraft	$9.95
3966	Collector's Guide to **Inkwells**, Identification & Values, Badders	$18.95
3881	Collector's Guide to **Novelty Radios**, Bunis/Breed	$18.95
4652	Collector's Guide to **Transistor Radios**, 2nd Ed., Bunis	$16.95
4653	Collector's Guide to **TV Memorabilia**, 1960s–1970s, Davis/Morgan	$24.95
2276	**Decoys**, Kangas	$24.95
1629	**Doorstops**, Identification & Values, Bertoia	$9.95
4567	Figural **Napkin Rings**, Gottschalk & Whitson	$18.95
3968	**Fishing Lure** Collectibles, Murphy/Edmisten	$24.95
3817	**Flea Market Trader**, 10th Ed., Huxford	$12.95
3976	Foremost Guide to **Uncle Sam** Collectibles, Czulewicz	$24.95
4641	**Garage Sale & Flea Market Annual**, 4th Ed.	$19.95
3819	**General Store Collectibles**, Wilson	$24.95
4643	**Great American West** Collectibles, Wilson	$24.95
2215	Goldstein's **Coca-Cola** Collectibles	$16.95
3884	Huxford's Collectible **Advertising**, 2nd Ed.	$24.95
2216	**Kitchen Antiques**, 1790–1940, McNerney	$14.95
3321	Ornamental & Figural **Nutcrackers**, Rittenhouse	$16.95
2026	**Railroad** Collectibles, 4th Ed., Baker	$14.95
1632	**Salt & Pepper Shakers**, Guarnaccia	$9.95
1888	**Salt & Pepper Shakers** II, Identification & Value Guide, Book II, Guarnaccia	$14.95
2220	**Salt & Pepper Shakers** III, Guarnaccia	$14.95
3443	**Salt & Pepper Shakers** IV, Guarnaccia	$18.95
4555	**Schroeder's Antiques Price Guide**, 14th Ed., Huxford	$12.95
2096	**Silverplated Flatware**, Revised 4th Edition, Hagan	$14.95
1922	Standard **Old Bottle** Price Guide, Sellari	$14.95
4708	Summers' Guide to **Coca-Cola**	$19.95
3892	**Toy & Miniature Sewing Machines**, Thomas	$18.95
3828	Value Guide to **Advertising Memorabilia**, Summers	$18.95
3977	Value Guide to **Gas Station** Memorabilia, Summers & Priddy	$24.95
3444	**Wanted to Buy**, 5th Edition	$9.95

This is only a partial listing of the books on antiques that are available from Collector Books. All books are well illustrated and contain current values. Most of these books are available from your local bookseller, antique dealer, or public library. If you are unable to locate certain titles in your area, you may order by mail from COLLECTOR BOOKS, P.O. Box 3009, Paducah, KY 42002-3009. Customers with Visa or MasterCard may phone in orders from 7:00–5:00 CST, Monday–Friday, Toll Free 1-800-626-5420. Add $2.00 for postage for the first book ordered and $0.30 for each additional book. Include item number, title, and price when ordering. Allow 14 to 21 days for delivery.

Schroeder's
ANTIQUES
Price Guide

. . . is the #1 best-selling antiques & collectibles value guide on the market today, and here's why . . .

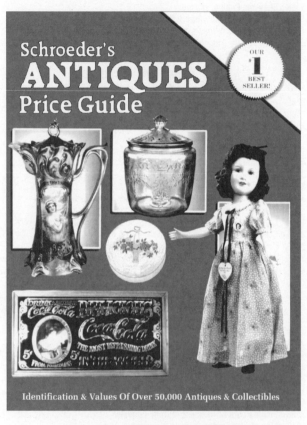

8½ x 11, 608 Pages, $12.95

• *More than 300 advisors, well-known dealers, and top-notch collectors work together with our editors to bring you accurate information regarding pricing and identification.*

• *More than 45,000 items in almost 500 categories are listed along with hundreds of sharp original photos that illustrate not only the rare and unusual, but the common, popular collectibles as well.*

• *Each large close-up shot shows important details clearly. Every subject is represented with histories and background information, a feature not found in any of our competitors' publications.*

• *Our editors keep abreast of newly developing trends, often adding several new categories a year as the need arises.*

If it merits the interest of today's collector, you'll find it in *Schroeder's*. And you can feel confident that the information we publish is up to date and accurate. Our advisors thoroughly check each category to spot inconsistencies, listings that may not be entirely reflective of market dealings, and lines too vague to be of merit. Only the best of the lot remains for publication.

Without doubt, you'll find
SCHROEDER'S ANTIQUES PRICE GUIDE
the only one to buy for
reliable information and values.

COLLECTOR BOOKS
A Division of Schroeder Publishing Co., Inc.